AF499276

THE GOSPEL ACCORDING TO THUNDER JOHNSON

A Re-telling of the Gospel of John by John in Cowboy Language

PERRY CRISP

LUCIDBOOKS

The Gospel According to Thunder Johnson: A Re-telling of the Gospel of John by John in Cowboy Language

Copyright © 2026 by Perry Crisp

Published by Lucid Books in Houston, TX
www.LucidBooks.com

All rights reserved. No part of this publication may be reproduced, stored in a retrieval system, or transmitted in any form by any means, electronic, mechanical, photocopy, recording, or otherwise, without the prior permission of the publisher, except as provided for by USA copyright law.

Unless otherwise indicated, scripture quotations are taken from the Scripture quotations marked (NKJV) are taken from the New King James Version®. Copyright © 1982 by Thomas Nelson. Used by permission. All rights reserved.

ISBN: 979-8-90344-401-4
eISBN: 979-8-90344-025-2

Special Sales: Most Lucid Books titles are available in special quantity discounts. Custom imprinting or excerpting can also be done to fit special needs. Contact Lucid Books at Info@LucidBooks.com

To my wife, Dorinda, whose gentle nudging gave me the courage to share this work with those who need to meet Jesus through Thunder Johnson.

CONTENTS

INTRODUCTION

What would it be like to sit down with the Apostle John, the one Jesus referred to as a "son of thunder," and listen to his gospel story first-hand? For that to happen, a few miracles must occur. First, the miracle of time travel. John has been in Heaven for over 1,900 years. Second, the miracle of language. John was fluent in Aramaic, Greek, and possibly Hebrew, but English wasn't even a language yet when he was alive. Third, the miracle of culture. John's culture of flowing robes, stringent laws, and living under the occupation and harsh rule of Rome is vastly different from blue jeans, moral relativism, and liberty.

The only way for these miracles to occur is through an author's imagination. That is what you have here. You're about to experience the miracle of time travel. In this story, the Apostle John travels from 100 AD to share his eyewitness account of the life of Jesus with us—his gospel account. However, his time machine stopped short of today and landed him in America in the 1850's. That means we will need to do a bit of our own time travel and go back 170 plus years to the days of the old west in America.

To *hear* John's gospel story, you must *become* part of the story. Slip on a worn pair of boots and jeans and put on a western shirt, vest, cowboy hat, and an ample supply of imagination and let's travel back in time to hear the world's greatest story straight from the horse's mouth . . . so to speak.

MEET THUNDER JOHNSON

An afternoon ride was just what you needed. It even seemed your horse enjoyed stretching her legs for a while. It had been quite an unusual couple of days. Somehow, you went from sleeping in your bed in your time period and waking up in an old cabin in 1855. No one was there but you and the aforementioned horse. There was an old iron bed, a sack of dried beans, a pot on a stove, a change of old western clothes (in your size), hay and saddle for the horse, and a poor-looking garden. You kept thinking you would wake up from this strange dream, but it had been two days and nights, and you were still alone in a cabin, feeling like you were in a cowboy movie. After two days, you decided to have a look around. You saddled the horse and rode the afternoon away.

You decide it's time to head back to the cabin. But as you try to turn the horse toward the cabin, her head and ears perk up suddenly. Something caught her attention.

A sound or a scent. A short detour won't make much difference, so off you ride in the direction of whatever caught your horse's attention and raised your curiosity.

You soon come across an elderly man gathering wood, preparing a fire for a meal. Without even looking up at you, he invites you to join him. As he motions toward his makeshift camp, you notice three others sitting around what is about to become a campfire. Their horses are tethered nearby, so you dismount and tether yours. The whole scene is a bit out of the ordinary. The other three have the same look on their faces as you assume covers yours. But they aren't looking at you. They're gawking at the elderly man building a fire. He is, to say the least, far from ordinary. His clothes are tattered and worn out. They aren't like any clothes you've ever seen. His accent is unlike any you've ever heard. It's almost as if he is speaking a different language, but you understand him with ease.

He introduces himself as Thunder Johnson and acts as though he has been waiting for you and the others. As Thunder takes a seat on the opposite side of the campfire from the rest of you, each of you begins to fire off questions that have been rolling around through your minds since you sat down. Thunder smiles, puts up a hand to stop the questions, and says, "I'd like to tell you a story if you've got time." He points to four coffee cups sitting near the edge of the fire and says, "Grab some coffee and sit for a spell. I came a long way and have a lot to say."

Sensing something mysterious and unique about this man, you all follow his suggestion. As you and the others reach for a cup, he leans toward you and says, "This is a story unlike any you've ever heard. No doubt, it'll be the most important story you ever hear. It took place in a land and time far removed. They spoke different in that place and time. They dressed different, too. But, no matter when or where you're from, this story is meant for you. It's a story I wrote a long time ago. I'm in this story, too, but it wasn't proper back then for the writer to spell out his own name, so I never name myself. But you can probably figure out who I am as I tell the story because I tend to get a lump in my throat. So, sit back and relax while I use your words to tell my story—and His."

Before you can stop yourself, you blurt out another question, "How could a story from some foreign land and ancient time mean anything to me? What do you call this story?"

The strange old man smiles, closes one eye, looks up at the trees, and says (as if announcing it to the whole world), "This is the Gospel According to Thunder Johnson!"

CHAPTER ONE

THE BEST CUT FROM GOD'S HERD

1-5 There was a time when nothing, including time, existed but Him. Before the sun ever set its saddle on the back of the mountains, He was already there. He and God rode the far-away places together as one. Yep, He was there before there were ever any pastures, ponies, or planets. When everything did get made, it was Him who brought it into being. Nothing has ever been unless it came from Him, including life. Life comes from Him and through Him. When you know Him, you can figure out life and see where you're headed because of the light that comes from His life. His light can shine into the darkest of skulls with no fear of it being snuffed out.

6-13 There was a cowboy sent from God by the name of Johnnie. Johnnie partnered with God to help folks see the Light. Truth is—God wanted everybody to cotton to the

Light. Now, Johnnie wasn't the Light. He just came to point other folks to the Light. This ain't no puny light. This Light shines brighter than a million campfires—Light enough for the whole world! This Fella we're talking about (the Light), visited this world He made, but no one knew Him. He even bunked with His own folks, and very few cottoned to Him. But to them that did, He showed them how to become one of God's own kin just by believing in His name. This ain't no normal way of becoming kin. It didn't happen by nature or man. These folk were born by God.

14-15 He wrapped Himself in human hide and rode with us. We 'ciphered He was different right from the start—like He was a reflection of something plum full o' tenderness and honesty. Johnnie got downright giddy when he told us about Him, "This is the One I was tellin' y'all about when I said, 'There's a Fella coming up the trail behind me that's a lot more important than I am. He's not following me . . . I'm gonna fall in behind Him!'"

16-18 Johnnie was right. We all felt like we had a hole in the pocket of our lives, but this Fella patched that hole real good. He more than patched it; He filled it with stuff we didn't deserve. Moses of way-back-when gave us the bare standards of how we ought to live in the Good Book, but we never knew what tenderness and honesty felt like until we met this Fella. His given name is Jesus. We soon discovered He was the Promised One known as the Christ. I reckon no man has ever laid eyes on God, but God does have one lone Son, who knows the Father above like no one else. He showed us what God is like.

19-23 This is how Johnnie recollects the way it started: A group of religious folk sent out a committee of uppity religious types from Jerusalem to ask Johnnie, "Who are you?" He was straight with them when he answered, "I ain't the Promised One we've all been looking for."

"Well," they asked again, "Then who are you? Are you Elijer?"

"Nope," answered Johnnie.

"Are you the Messenger?" they asked.

Johnnie shook his head.

They were starting to get flustered and said, "Mister, we got folk waiting on us for an answer. What are we supposed to tell 'em?"

"Tell 'em this," he said. "I'm a voice hollering in the woods, 'Blaze a trail for the Lord,' just like the messenger Isaiah said."

24-28 This bunch that asked all the questions had joined themselves up with the top religious outfit of their time, the Literalists. They asked Johnnie, "Why are you baptizing if you ain't the Promised One or any of them other fellas?"

Johnnie let out a sigh and answered, "All I'm doing is baptizing with water. You ain't seen nothing yet. He's out there, and you don't even know it. That's right! The Promised

One is coming right up the trail behind me! You don't need to worry none about me. He's the One you better get ready for. Shoot, I'm not worthy enough to take His boots off."

This all happened down in a place called Bethany near the Jordan River, where Johnnie was holding baptizing services.

29-34 The very next day, Johnnie looked up and saw Jesus riding toward him. He smiled and yelled, "Look yonder! That's the best cut from God's own herd, and He's gonna run sin right out of town! He's the One I told y'all about, the Fella coming up the trail behind me that I'm fixing to follow the rest o' my days. I never had no face-to-face with Him, but I was sent up the trail ahead of Him to introduce Him to the world. That's what all this baptizing has been about."

Then Johnnie saw something with his own eyes and told the folks what he was seeing, "I saw what looked like a dove, only it was the Heaven-Spirit. The Heaven-Spirit lit on Him and stayed there. Like I said, I never seen Him before, but I knew it was Him because the One who sent me out baptizing told me, 'When you see the Heaven-Spirit come down and land on a Fella, you'll know He's the One who baptizes with the Holy Spirit.' And I can tell you for true—this Fella IS the Son of God!"

35-42 The next day, Johnnie was jawing with a couple of fellas that had been riding with him when he saw Jesus ride by. Johnnie nodded his head toward Jesus and said, "Look, fellas. The Best Cut from God's own herd!" Those two fellas tipped their hats to Johnnie, eased into their saddles and fell in behind Jesus.

Jesus turned and saw they were following and said, "Can I help you?"

They said, "Sir, we was just wondering where You're headed."

Jesus smiled and said, "Come on. I'll show you."

They joined up with Him and spent all morning together. One of them was named Andy, who had a brother named Pete. Andy left Jesus's company just long enough to fetch his brother Pete and tell him, "We have found the Promised One."

Andy brought his brother to Jesus. When Jesus first set eyes on Pete, He said, "You're John's boy. I'm gonna call you Rocky."

43-50 Jesus needed to head toward Galilee Territory, so the next day they all hit the trail in that direction. When they got there, Jesus found a fella named Phil and said, "Join Me." Phil was from the same town Andy and Rocky were from—Bethsaida.

Phil had a bud named Nate, and he told Nate about Jesus, "You'll never guess who we found! We found the One that ole Moses writ about in the Good Book (same Fella the old-timers mentioned): Jesus, Joe's boy from Nazareth!"

Nate shook his head, "I ain't never heard o' nothing worth spit coming out of Nazareth."

Phil shrugged, "Come see for yourself."

Jesus peered from under the brim of His hat and watched Nate walk toward Him. It seemed as though Jesus was glad to see Nate, as if He'd already known him.

Jesus said, "Now fellas, what we have here is a genuine cowboy without an ounce of dishonesty in his bones."

Nate was shocked, "How'd you know about me?"

"I saw you taking a nap under that shade tree before Phil ever approached you," answered Jesus.

"Sir," said Nate as he dropped to one knee, "You are the real deal. You've got to be the Son of God!"

Jesus chuckled, "You're convinced just because I told you I seen you under that shade tree? You ain't seen nothing yet!"

Then Jesus said, "Let me make you a promise: Your eyes are gonna be privy to some amazing sights. You're gonna see Heaven's gate flung wide open and the angels of God rising and falling on the Son of Man."

CHAPTER TWO

Y'ALL DO ANYTHING HE SAYS

1-8 Right after that, Jesus's mama had to go to a wedding in Cana (Galilee Territory). Jesus and His tag-alongs were invited, too. The wedding hit a snag when they ran out of wine. Of course, Jesus's mama knew what her Son could and should do, so she told Him, "They're out of wine."

"I don't see what that has to do with Me, Momma," Jesus whispered. "Besides, it ain't My time yet."

His momma paid no attention to what He said. Instead, she went over to the servers, pointed them in the direction of her Son, and said, "Y'all do anything He says."

Jesus shook His head at His momma's meddling, looked around, and found six big ole wash tubs that could hold near thirty gallons. He told the servers, "Take these here wash tubs and fill 'em up." They filled them plum full of water.

Then Jesus took His canteen and handed it to one of the servers, "Draw a canteen full out of one of them wash tubs and take it to the head server." They did.

9-12 The head server took a sip of that water; only it wasn't water anymore! It was wine! He had no idea where it came from or what had happened (but the servers knew). The head server hollered at the fella getting hitched and said, "Normally, folks bring the good stuff out first, and then when everybody's plastered, they start hauling out the sorry stuff. But I got to hand it to you—you saved the best 'til last!"

Jesus pulled His first miracle in Cana, Galilee Territory. He really showed His stuff, and His tag-alongs were becoming more and more convinced that Jesus was the Promised One. After that, Jesus spent a few days with His momma, His brothers, and His tag-alongs down by the lake in a town called Capernaum.

13-17 It was nearly time for a famous Big Religious Holiday, so Jesus headed to Jerusalem. When He arrived, He stopped off at the church-house and went inside. He was disgusted by what He saw. Peddlers and auctioneers were doing business everywhere. Jesus went back to His horse and got a rope. He lassoed table after table and jerked them to the ground. He ran every man and critter out of the church-house. With a square jaw and a firm tone, Jesus told them, "Get this stuff out of here! Stop turning My Father's house into a flea market!"

The fellas that were tagging along with Jesus remembered words from the Good Book: "Passion for the house of God will be branded into My soul."(Quote from Psalm 69:9)

18-25 So the religious folks questioned Jesus about His antics, "Can you give us one good reason why you think you have the right to come in here and do what you done?"

Jesus took a deep breath and answered with a calm voice, "Take down this house and I'll bring it back up in three days."

The religious folk got smart aleck and said, "This house took forty-six years to build! How could the likes of you bring it back up in three days?"

But Jesus wasn't talking about the church-house; He meant His own body. So, when that did happen, and Jesus did rise up out of that grave, the fellas following Him had an inspired recollection of the time when He said these words. They were convinced of the Good Book and this here statement that Jesus made.

While Jesus was in Jerusalem for the Big Religious Holiday, lots of folks cottoned to Him when they saw the miracles He was doing. But Jesus didn't let Himself get won over by their liking. He knew what folk were like. He didn't need a soul to tell Him about that. He knew what folk were made of, better than anyone.

CHAPTER THREE

HOW TO MEET YOUR MAKER

1-8 Late one night after the Big Religious Holiday, a top bull rider and Legalist named Nick came to His campfire to chat.

"Partner," he said, "We all know that You are a bronc buster come from God to teach us all. Nobody can ride the way You do unless God's in the saddle with Him." Jesus leaned toward the campfire, stirred the coals, looked right into Nick's eyes and said, "Listen to me, cowboy. Unless you are born again, you'll never ride in the great "by-and-by."

"Born again?" The old bull rider pulled his hat off and scratched his head. He had to think on that one a spell. He moved his tobacco to the other jaw, spat into the coals of the campfire, and asked, "How can an old man be born again? I can't climb back into my maw's holding pin and bust out the gate again. That's nonsense!"

Jesus chuckled and shook His head. "I'm not talking about having two physical births. I'm talking about ONE physical birth and ONE spiritual birth. Without that second one, you'll never qualify for the final round."

Jesus leaned back against His bedroll and explained. "Flesh comes from flesh (hide from hide)—just like you came from your maw. But your spirit is dead, and it can only be born to life by God's Spirit. Don't act so surprised about needing a spiritual birth. It's no different than the wind. You hear it, but you can't put your finger on it. Same with Spirit-born folk."

9-17 Now Nick was leaning toward the fire, playing with a stick. He shook his head and said, "I don't get it. I just don't understand this."

Jesus smiled at him and said, "You, a Legalist AND a top bull rider on the pro circuit—and you don't know beans about how to meet your Maker? Nick, I'm telling you what I know and what I've seen, but you're still skeptical. If you're having trouble believing me about everyday things on Earth, how are you ever going to 'cipher the truth when I tell you what goes on in Heaven? I'm the only one that's been there."

Jesus leaned toward Nick and took the stick away from him to get him to look at Him as He said, "You remember how ole Moses raised up that snake on a stick back in the old days? One of these days, your fellow religious types are going to form a posse and come hunting Me. When they find Me, they're going to string Me up. But that's alright—cause when I'm lifted up, anyone who believes in Me will live forever with God. For God loves every cowboy and cowgirl so much that He took from His own stock and gave His only sired Son, that whoever believes in Him should not bite the big one, but live forever with Him."

Jesus put a hand on Nick's shoulder and said, "Nick, God didn't send me here to call off the rodeo. He sent me here to save the cowboy."

Did Nicodemus really become a believer? We see him at the tomb of Jesus in John 19:39 bringing spices for Jesus's burial . . . an act normally provided by family. I can see ole Nick standing there by the tomb of Jesus with his cowboy hat over his heart. I can hear him say . . .

"*Good-bye partner. You've changed my life forever. I know that one day I will ride with You again. Because of You, I stand taller in my saddle knowing that You have prepared a place for me at the great rodeo arena of Heaven. I never knew what life was until You led me to that second birth. You were right. They came after You and strung You up. But before they did, You made a believer out of me and a bunch of others.*

"I have a feeling it's not over yet. If anybody can whoop death and come out riding again, it'll be You. Thank You, Jesus, for saving this ole cowboy."

18-20 Jesus continued long into the night with Nick, "If a man believes in Me, he won't stand trial before God. But any man that don't believe in Me has already been tried and found guilty because he chose not to believe in the name of God's one and only Son.

"The sad fact is, Nick, everybody likes the dark instead of the light. I'm here as a light. But people want darkness so they can hide what they're doing. When a cowboy is up to no good, he don't want to get found out, so if he sees a campfire, he rides around it. But a cowboy with nothing to hide is thrilled at the sight of a fire and not ashamed to come toward it."

22-24 After this, Jesus took His tag-alongs on a ride through the countryside of Judea. They spent some time together and even did some baptizing along the way. Johnnie was doing some baptizing himself in a little place called Aenon, which is near Salim. It was about the best watering hole he could find, and folks were coming and getting baptized (of course, this was before Johnnie got thrown in jail).

25-36 Some of Johnnie's fellas got tangled up arguing with a religious type about his legalistic view of what makes a man clean on the inside.

They brought their argument to Johnnie and said, "Sir, the Fella you told us about that we saw you with over by the Jordan, is baptizing—and folks are coming His way in droves!"

Johnnie used this as an opportunity to set a few things

straight, "You don't get one cotton-picking thing unless it comes from Heaven. Y'all know what I told you. I ain't the Promised One. I just came up the trail ahead of Him.'"

The dumb look on their faces let Johnnie know he needed to do some more explaining. "The fella that gets the girl for his bride is called the groom. But the groom's best friend, his partner who he's waiting to hear from, lets out a shout when he hears the groom's voice. Don't you see? I can't be any happier about this! It's time for Him to come to the center of the arena, and it's time for me to ride off quiet-like."

Johnnie looked up at the sky, "If you come from up there, you're way above everybody else." Then he bent down and picked up some dirt, "But if you're from down here, then down here is all you know and all you can talk about." Johnnie looked back up and smiled, "Jesus is from up there, so He rides taller than any of us. He's going to tell us what He knows, but nobody from down here will swallow it much. But if a fella does believe what He says, he'll learn just how true God is. God sent Him down here. So, when He talks, He says exactly what God would say to us, holding nothing back. God's given Him free rein. The Father loves His Son and trusts Him to get the job done."

Johnnie rubbed the back of his neck and squinted his eyes at the horizon, "The fella that believes in the Son will ride tall and live forever, but the fella that stubbornly refuses to believe in Him will forever be saddle sore and won't ever find life; all he'll ever find is the never-ending anger of God chewing on his backside for refusing what God was offering."

CHAPTER FOUR

YOUR THIRST KEEPS COMING BACK

1-6 Now, Jesus wasn't really doing the baptizing. It was His tag-alongs. But Jesus knew that the Literalists had gotten wind that His herd of followers was growing and folks were being baptized, so He left Judea and rode back to Galilee Territory. But He didn't take the normal trail. He set off through the Samaritan Nation. He and His tag-alongs stopped just at the edge of a town called Sychar in Samaria, close to where Jake of old gave his son, Joe, a fair section of land (it's all there in the Good Book). Jake's well was at hand, and Jesus was tuckered out from the long ride. He got off His horse and sat down at the well. A glance at the sky told Him it was about six o'clock in the evening time.

7-12 About that time, a Samaritan female riding bareback came to get some water from the well. She saw the strange cowboy, but didn't say anything to Him. Nor did she expect a peep out of Him. Samaritans and Judeans didn't mix. She was about to be surprised.

"Ma'am, fetch me a drink," Jesus said. He'd already sent His tag-alongs into town for some grub.

"Mister, you ain't from around here. Don't you know your type ain't supposed to have no dealings with my type? Why would you ask me for a drink?" she asked. (See? I told you Judeans and Samaritans didn't mix).

Jesus managed a slight grin and said, "If you really knew who you were talking to, or had any clue at all about God's gift to you, you'd be asking Me for a drink, and I'd give you living water."

"Mister," she said, "I hate to bust your bubble, but you're perched on a very deep well without a bucket. How do you suppose you're gonna fetch me this 'living water'? Don't tell me! You're so great, you could even put ole Jake to shame. He dug this well and drank from it himself; he and all his kin and livestock."

13-19 Jesus wasn't shaken by her fiery tone. He calmly answered, "True. But you have to keep coming back to this well because your thirst keeps coming back. The water I have in mind for you will make it where you're never thirsty again! Once you get ahold of the water I'm offering, you won't need a well because you'll become one! You'll have water gushing up from inside forever."

"Mister," she said with a deep yearning, "Fetch me some

of this kind of water you're talking about so I don't have to keep coming back here."

"Alright," agreed Jesus, "You go get your husband and meet Me back here."

"I ain't got a husband," she said.

"No, you don't. You're right," said Jesus. "As a matter of fact, you've already been through five husbands, and the fella you're with now isn't even yours. You've been honest with Me, ma'am."

"Mister, I can tell You're a man of God."

20-24 She had a spiritual issue that had been festering inside her, "My people have always worshipped here on this mountain, but Your people believe the only place a body can worship is in Jerusalem."

Jesus spoke to her spiritual issue, "Ma'am, trust Me. There'll come a time when God won't be worshipped in either place. Your people don't know what you're worshipping. The only reason My people know is because God chose to reveal His saving plan through them. But a time is coming, and it's here right now, when the genuine lovers of God will worship Him personally inside themselves, with sincerity and honesty. Yes ma'am, that's the kind of worship God wants. God is Spirit, so if you want to worship Him, you gotta worship Him in spirit an' truth."

25-26 The woman was thirsty for more, "I believe in the Promised One. When He comes, He'll set us all straight."

"Well, ma'am," Jesus said. "I reckon you're talking to Him."

27-37 About that time, His tag-alongs came back. They couldn't figure out why He was talking to a woman. But they kept their traps shut. The woman left her bucket, hopped on her horse, and rode like lightning into town to tell folks what just happened.

"Hurry up, y'all! Come see this Fella who knows everything there is to know about me," she told them. "I got a hunch He could be the Promised One!" Some of the town folks headed toward Jesus.

While they were coming, Jesus's tag-alongs were after Him to eat, "Teacher, eat! You need Your strength."

"Nope. Not hungry," He said. "I've got vittles none of you know about." The tag-alongs whispered to each other, "You think somebody else brought Him some grub?"

Jesus heard them discussing it and said, "My hunger is satisfied by doing what My Father sent Me here to do. Most folks believe harvest time is still four months out." The tag-alongs thought Jesus was changing the subject, but He wasn't.

"I'll tell you what," He continued. "Pop your eyes open and take a look-see. Them fields are ready right now. The farmer has already earned his keep. He's gathering up eternal ripe stuff right now, and the farmer that went before him and sowed the seed has joined him in the celebrating. I'm seeing this come true right before My eyes with these Samaritans."

Jesus was enjoying the sight as He said, "'One fella plants the seeds and another fella brings in the crops.' I sent you to fetch what you haven't even worked for. Someone else did all the work, and their work fills your stomachs."

39-42 That Samaritan female told lots of folks about her conversation with Jesus, and quite a few of them believed He was the Promised One. They all approached Jesus and invited Him to stick around. So, He stayed there another couple of days. The number of those who believed in Him grew as He continued to talk about the things of God.

They told the woman who first met Jesus, "At first, we believed in Him because of what happened to you. But not now. We done heard it for ourselves and have no doubt that He really is the One who has come to save the world."

43-45 When the two days were up, Jesus rode out of town and headed for Galilee Territory. Jesus had already let it be known that a cowboy doesn't get much respect on his own ranch. When they rode into Galilee Territory, the reception was overwhelming. Many of the Galileans had attended the Big Religious Holiday and saw some of the amazing things He did there.

46-54 Jesus also returned to Cana, the town where He'd performed the wine miracle. While in Cana, a big-time rancher's boy in Capernaum got sick. When the rancher found out that Jesus was in Galilee Territory, he hurried to Him and begged Him to ride down to Capernaum to help his young-un. The boy was on his deathbed.

Jesus told the man, "Y'all just want Me to work miracles or you won't believe."

"Mister," the rancher said, "I beg You to ride down with me before my little boy dies!"

"Get on your horse and ride," said Jesus. "Your boy's gonna be alright." The man was convinced that Jesus was telling the truth, so he got on his horse and headed home. While he was still on his way down the mountain, some of his cowhands met him with the news that his boy had taken a turn for the better. The rancher asked his hands what time it was when the boy started feeling better.

"Yesterday, about sun-up, the fever broke," they answered. The boy's dad knew that was the exact time that Jesus told him his son would live. Right then and there the rancher really believed that Jesus was the Promised One, and so did everyone on his spread. That made two miracles by Jesus after He left Judea to go to Galilee Territory.

CHAPTER FIVE

A RACE OF SICK FOLKS

1-5 Jesus headed back to Jerusalem for another religious event with His people. Over by the stockades in Jerusalem, there was a large spring-fed pond surrounded by five gazebos. Rumor was that an angel would occasionally stir up the water in that pond, giving it healing powers. But there was only enough healing power for one person at a time. So naturally, when the water stirred, it became a race of sick folks all clambering and crawling toward the pond to get there first. Sick folk of all kind waited by that pond all day every day. One fella had been sick for thirty-eight years.

6-13 Jesus happened by there and seen that ole boy. He knew he'd been bad off for a long time. Jesus asked him if he was tired of being sick and if he was ready for a change, "You want to get well?"

"Mister," he answered. "I got nobody to put me into the

pond when the water gets stirred up. 'Fore I can ever get near the water, somebody always gets there ahead o' me."

"Here's what I want you to do," Jesus said. "I want you to get up on your feet, gather up your bedroll, and walk!" Just like that, the man was healed. A big ole grin snaked all over his face as he looked at Jesus. He bent over, picked up his bedroll, and started walking and kicking his heels.

It just so happened that the man was healed on a holy day. Some of the religious types seen the man toting his bed roll. They got all legalistic with him and reminded him it was a holy day, "It's against the law for you to tote your bed roll!"

"I'm only doing what the Man who healed me told me to do. He said, 'Gather up your bed roll, and walk.'"

"What fella told you to gather up your bed roll and walk?" they demanded. The healed fella shrugged his shoulders. He didn't know who the Man was that done the healing because Jesus had blended into the crowd shortly after the fact.

14-17 Later, Jesus found the healed man in the church-house and said, "Look at you! You're all healed up. Stay off the sin trail. You don't want to end up worse off than you were."

The healed man went and told the religious types that the Fella who healed him was Jesus. It riled the religious types that Jesus would do such things on a holy day. Jesus really got Himself on their bad side.

But it didn't bother Jesus none, "As long as My Father is working, I'mma keep on working."

18 Now, this really made the hair stand up on the necks of them religious folks. Not only was Jesus ignoring holy day laws, He was claiming God as His own Father (which would make Jesus of equal stock with God).

19-23 Jesus kept on, "I'll tell you what: I don't do a thing on My own. I just do what I see My Father doing. I'm just a mirror image, reflecting Him. My Father loves Me and enjoys showing Me what He's doing. And He's only just begun. You ain't seen nothing yet!

"Just like My Father can bring a dead man back to life, I've got the same power to give life to whoever I want. Now, I know you're gonna bark at what I'm about to say, but the truth is: My Father has even given over His judicial duties to Me, so you best be aware that however you figure on treating My Father, you better treat Me the same. If you don't respect Me, you don't respect Him.

24-30 "I guarantee," Jesus continued. "If a fella listens to what I have to say and wraps his heart around the One who sent Me, he'll live forever and won't have to worry none about Judgment Day. He'll just pass right on through to eternity in Heaven the second he kicks the bucket.

"Let there be no doubt: A time is coming, and it's on us right now, when the dead can hear the voice of the Son of God; an' those that hear will live. The Father holds life in His hands, and He's passed that ability to His Son, as well. He's also given His Son the ability to make decisions based on His knowledge of what's in a man's heart. It's perfectly fitting because He's familiar with both worlds.

"Don't throw a shoe just because I said dead folks will hear My voice soon and will leave their graves. The ones that have gone down the right trail will follow it on up to a second chance at living forever. But those who've ridden the trail of evil will find themselves facing Me on Judgment Day.

"I don't make judgments on My own. I just listen to the One who sent Me and follow His heart and it can't be wrong because I get everything from Him.

31-40 "If it was all about Me, and I was bragging and carrying on about Myself, I wouldn't be worth listening to. But there's Another who can verify what I'm saying, and I know His words are straight and true.

"Y'all had Me checked out by Johnnie, the Baptizer. He spoke the truth about Me. Not that a man's testimony makes much difference to Me, but I'm telling you this in hopes that it'll lead you to the right trail.

"Johnnie's campfire burned bright for a while. Y'all were all drawn to it at one time. But I'm here to pick up where he left off, and My Father's given Me the firepower to do it with. And I'm gonna get it done. The stuff I'm doing right before your eyes is proof that the Father sent Me here.

"My Father has even tried to tell you about Me Himself, but y'all ain't in a listening mood. And you couldn't see Him if you tried. You may have His Word in your head, but it's never found its way to your heart. Otherwise, you'd be convinced that I came because He sent Me. The sad thing is, you fiddle constantly with the Good Book because you know that's where the secret to living forever can be found. But My life, My purpose, and My truth are written all over the Good Book and you still can't see it. You stubbornly refuse to follow Me even though I'm blazing the only trail to eternal life.

41-47 "I'm not asking for man's applause—But I know you inside and out, and there ain't an ounce of love for God inside you!

"I'm here representing My Father, but that ain't good enough for you. Let anybody else ride into town tooting his own horn and y'all would be patting him on the back.

"I can't figure out how you're ever gonna believe what I'm telling you. You impress the snot out of each other, but you turn up your noses at any attempt to look for the glory that comes from the One and Only God.

"Don't fret over whether I'll make accusations against you to My Father. You've set yourselves up under ole Moses with enough rope to hang yourselves.

"If you really understood ole Moses, you would understand Me, because we ride the same trail. He even wrote about Me in the Good Book. But I doubt you'll ever believe anything I say if you've never followed what ole Moses wrote."

CHAPTER SIX

STRAIGHT FROM HEAVEN'S KITCHEN

1-3 After His confrontation with the religious types, Jesus took a boat across Lake Galilee. The more miracles Jesus did to heal the sick, the larger the herd of folks that wanted to get next to Him. So, Jesus and His usual tag-alongs rode up into the hills for a getaway.

4-6 The Big Religious Holiday and all its events were still going on, and Jesus was the talk of the town. Jesus had been getting some shut-eye while relaxing under a shade tree with His hat resting on the bridge of His nose. He peered out from under the brim of His hat and saw a great big bunch of folks coming up the hill toward Him.

Without sitting up, Jesus asked Phil, "Any idea where we can get some bread or something so all those folks coming up the hill can eat?" Jesus already knew what He was gonna do. He just wanted to see Phil's reaction.

7-10 Phil saw the size of the crowd and nearly jumped out of his boots, "It'd take pert near a year's wages just to give ever' person a bite."

Pete's brother, Andy, had an idea. He told Jesus, "There's a young-un here with five sandwiches and a couple o' sticks of beef jerky. That's a lot for a boy, but it ain't much for this hungry herd."

Jesus told His tag-alongs, "Get everybody to sit down." If it were a herd of horses instead of people, they wouldn't have had a problem because there was plenty of grass for them to sit on. Just counting the men-folk, there was close to 5,000 head.

11-15 Jesus took the young-un's sandwiches, said grace, and sent it out to the crowd. He did the same with the jerky. As long as they were hungry, He kept sending more out. When everybody's belly was full, Jesus told His dozen tag-alongs, "Gather up the leftovers. Never waste a miracle." They hauled in twelve baskets of leftover sandwiches and jerky sticks from those who had eaten.

When the folks saw this, they knew, "He really is the Messenger sent from God to the world!" The more the people talked about what happened, the more they wanted to put a crown on Jesus's head and set Him up on a throne as king. But that wasn't part of the plan, so Jesus gave them the slip and found a quiet place further up the hill.

16-21 When it was dark, His tag-alongs went down to the lake, hopped into a boat, and headed across the lake toward Capernaum. They didn't know where Jesus was. He never came back after dinner. Halfway across the lake, the wind got up something fierce. The waves were a-churning. They fought the waves for nearly four miles when they saw Jesus takin' a stroll on top of the water! He was headed for the boat, and they looked like they'd seen a ghost.

But Jesus hollered, "It's Me! Stop shaking in your boots." They helped Jesus onto the boat and found themselves ashore in no time at the exact place they were trying to get to all along.

22-25 The next day, the folks that stayed on the other side of the lake knew that Jesus's bunch only had the one boat, and they saw His tag-alongs leave without Him. Other boats from Tiberius had come along close by where they ate the sandwiches. But they couldn't figure out where Jesus had run off to. One thing was obvious: Jesus and His tag-alongs weren't there anymore, so they hitched a boat ride to Capernaum to see if they could find Jesus.

They did. There He was on the other side of the lake! They were amazed as they stuttered to ask, "What? Where? How? When did You get here?"

26-31 Jesus stopped them before they could proceed with any attempt to make Him king, "Listen: You folks are scouring all over looking for Me for the wrong reasons. Not because you understand the signs behind the miracles, but because your bellies were filled and you're wanting seconds.

"You spend all your effort on stuff that won't last when you ought to be rolling up your sleeves for the good stuff that lasts forever, which I can supply because My Father approves."

"We ain't afraid of work. What do we need to do?" they asked.

Jesus said, "Here's what God wants you to do: Put every ounce of your faith in Me."

"Well, show us sumpin and when we see it, we'll do like You said." They continued, "What Ya gonna do? Our kinfolk ate Heaven-Bread in the desert, like it says in the Good Book: 'He fixed Heaven-Bread for them to eat.'" (Quote from Nehemiah 9:15)

32-40 Jesus answered, "I'll tell you what: Ole Moses wasn't the one supplying the Heaven-Bread. Only My Father has the true Heaven-Bread and only He can give it to you. This bread I'm talking 'bout is not what you're thinking. The true Heaven-Bread sent from God is the One who came from heaven and feeds the hungry soul by giving genuine life to the world."

They begged, "Mister, we want this bread for the rest of our lives."

"I'm the bread of life," Jesus answered. "I can't make it any clearer than that. You come to Me, your soul won't ever growl with hunger again; you believe in Me and your soul won't ever be parched again.

"But it's like I've been telling you: You're looking right at Me, but you still don't see who I am. It's all in My Father's hands. Whoever He sends Me is Mine forever. I'll never give anyone the boot. I'm not here to do My own thing. I came from heaven to do My Father's bidding. Here's what He wants Me to do: Keep all the folk He's given Me without losing a one of them and trot them all out alive and kicking on the last day. My Father also wants folk to see His Son and believe in Him so they can live forever and join in the celebrating at the end of time."

41-51 Of course, all this talk about being the bread of heaven didn't set too well with the religious types. They were arguing against any possibility by saying, "Ain't this Joe's boy? Jesus is a local. We know His parents! Now, He's trying to convince us that He came from heaven?"

Jesus interrupted, "Stop your belly-aching and listen. Unless My Father puts His lasso around your heart and delivers you to Me, you'll never see Me for who I truly am. But those who the Father has sent to Me, I will make sure they're good to go on the last day.

"One of the old-time messengers wrote it like this, 'They'll all get their learning from God.'(Quote from Isaiah 54:13) Everybody who has paid attention and got his learning from

My Father is sent to Me. Not that anyone actually sat in a school room and seen the Father with his own eyes. Only the One sent from God has seen the Father.

"I'll say it again: You believe, you live forever. I'm the bread of life. Your kinfolk ate the Heaven-Bread in the desert, and still ended up in a graveyard. The bread I'm telling you about is straight from Heaven's kitchen and anyone that eats it won't die. I'm the Living Heaven-Bread. Eat this bread; keep on living. To be more specific, the bread that I will give to bring real life to this world is My own hide."

52-58 That started another argument among the religious types, "He's asking us to chew on His hide?"

Jesus responded, "Like it or not, if you don't eat My flesh and swallow My blood, you'll die. But those who will eat My flesh and swallow My blood will live forever, and I will set them free at the last day, because I'm the only meal that'll keep your spiritual belly full.

"Don't you see? That way you live in Me because I live in you. My Father lives and I live because He sent Me, so whoever consumes Me will live for the same reason."

Jesus stood before them and spread out His arms and said, "This is the Heaven-Bread; it's different from what your kinfolk ate. They're all pushing up daisies now. Whoever will eat this Heaven-Bread will live forever."

59-65 Jesus taught the people these things in a church-house in Capernaum. It disturbed even some of His tag-alongs.

One of them asked, "Is anybody getting any of this? I'm stumped! Pardon the pun, but it's awfully hard to swallow!" They all shook their heads.

Jesus knew they were struggling with His words, and He asked, "Do My words offend you?" He continued, "Suppose you woke up tonight and saw Me rising up toward Heaven? Life comes from the Spirit, not the flesh. My words are spiritual and alive. Some of you are still not convinced." (Jesus already knew who wouldn't believe, and He knew who the back-stabber was).

He said, "Like I said already, you can't understand any of this until My Father unlocks your heart and gives you to Me."

66-71 Right then and there, a bunch of His followers stopped tagging along. Jesus spoke to the dozen that stayed with Him, "Anybody else wanna leave?"

Rocky answered, "And just where would we go? You're the only One who's filled with the true words of life. Besides, You've convinced us! We not only believe it—no man could talk us out of it: You are the Promised One from God!"

Jesus sighed and said, "I hand-picked all twelve of you, but one of you is riding for the devil." Judas, the son of Simon Iscariot, was the one Jesus was talking about because He knew Judas was fixing to hand Him over to the religious types.

CHAPTER SEVEN

WHY DO Y'ALL WANT ME DEAD?

1-9 The religious folk were mighty upset with Jesus's talk, so He figured it best to mosey on back to Galilee Territory for a spell. He was a wanted man in Judea (in the bad sense of the term). Now, there was a mighty important religious holiday taking place back in Jerusalem, so Jesus's brothers tried to talk Him into going back, "Get on back to Judea and show Your tag-alongs some more of what You can do. Why hide what ought to be public? If You've got all this power, why not show the world what You can do?" (Even His own kin had their doubts about Him).

Jesus answered, "It's bad timing for Me. But you fellas have nothing but time. You don't have any enemies out yonder, but I do because I won't keep quiet about the world's evil doings. Y'all go on up and have a good time celebrating the holiday. I'll stay here until I'm ready." So, Jesus stayed for a bit in Galilee Territory.

10-13 Jesus's brothers went on to the holiday celebration, and Jesus wasn't too far behind. But Jesus kind of snuck into Jerusalem, doing His best not to stick out like a sore thumb. The religious types had their eyes peeled for Him. They went all through the crowds and couldn't find Him. Jesus was the talk of the town. Some good, some bad. "He's a good ole boy," one fella would say. But another would pop off and say, "Shoot no! He's up to no good." Even with all this talk about Jesus, it was kept "hush-hush" because everyone was scared of the religious types.

14-20 Jesus laid low until the celebrating was about half-way done, then He made His way to the church-house to talk some more about God. He dazzled the religious types with His Good Book smarts, "How does He know the Good Book like that without even enrolling in none of our seminaries?"

Jesus answered, "My learning isn't from head knowledge. All I know I learned from the One who sent Me. If a fella really wants to be honest in 'ciphering God's will, he can take a look at what I'm saying and know if it's from God or if I'm just making it up.

"Anybody who just makes stuff up is looking for attention. All I want to do is honor the One who sent Me by being completely honest and open.

"Didn't ole Moses teach y'all the basic standards of

living? But y'all keep flunking the basics. Why do y'all want Me dead?"

"You're crazy," they responded. "Nobody said anything about killing You!"

21-24 "I did one miracle and everybody went nuts," Jesus answered. "Think on this: Ole Moses started a tradition, a certain religious ritual done to a man on the holy day. (Actually, it was Moses and some of your other kinfolk from way back). When a fella gets this ritual done on him on the holy day to keep from breaking Moses's tradition, how in the world are you gonna get mad at Me for completely healing a man on the holy day? Quit making up your mind based on what stuff looks like on the outside. Start using your noggin' for something besides a hat rack."

25-27 Some people in Jerusalem started talking, "Ain't this the Fella they're itching to string up? Look at Him! He's right there in front of God an' everybody talking away, and nobody's doing a cotton-picking thing to stop Him. Maybe what He's saying about Himself is true and the religious types know it! But how could He be the Promised One when we know where He growed up? We ain't supposed to know about His hometown."

28-31 As Jesus was teaching in the church-house, He answered back, "Y'all do know Me and where I'm from. That's true. But I was led here, and the One that led Me here is real. Y'all don't really know Him. I do because I came from Him. He sent Me."

At that point, they tried real hard to grab ahold of Jesus, but all they got was air. It wasn't time yet. In spite of the religious types' efforts to stop Jesus, more and more folk started lining up behind Him. They reasoned, "I don't reckon any other Promised One could do anywhere near the kinds of miracles this Fella's done."

32-36 The Literalists overheard this kind of talk about Jesus, so the uppity religious types teamed up with the Literalists and called the Marshall in to have Jesus arrested.

Jesus said, "I won't be around here much longer. I'm headed back to where I came from—to the One who sent Me here. Look all you want. You'll never find Me. You can't get there from here."

The religious folks said to each other, "Where's He planning on hiding so good we can't find Him? You don't reckon He'd sidle up to them highfalutin Greek snobs, do you? What does He mean, 'Look all you want; you'll never find Me; you can't get there from here'?"

37-39 On the last and most important day of the holiday season, Jesus stood in front of a crowd at the church-house and said, "Are you thirsty? Come get a drink! Ever who believes in Me, the Good Book says, you'll have an endless river flowing inside of you."

He was talking in spiritual ways. When a fella or a gal

chooses to believe in Jesus, the Spirit of God moves into that fella or gal. The Spirit hadn't made Himself known yet because He was waiting 'till Jesus took care of business.

40-49 When people heard Jesus say that about the endless river, they said, "He really is the Messenger from God!" Others said, "He's the Promised One!" But some were still scratching their head and saying, "Dog-gone-it, the Promised One don't come from Galilee Territory, does He? Don't the Good Book say the Promised One will come from the direct line of David and his hometown of Bethlehem?" The discussion over Jesus split the crowd in two. Some still wanted to jump Him, but no one laid a finger on Him.

The uppity religious types and Legalists met with the Marshall and asked, "Why ain't He in jail yet?"

The Marshall had a look of fear on his face and said, "I ain't never heard no man talk like He does."

The Legalists sneered at the Marshall and asked, "Has He pulled the wool over your eyes, too? Take a look around. Have any of us higher class, better educated folk bought what He's selling? Any Legalists joining His parade? But this crowd of numbskulls, ignorant of the Bare Standards, are a cursed lot!"

50-53 Nick, the fella that snuck in and had a talk with Jesus one night, being that he was one of them Legalists, spoke up. "Nowhere in the Bare Standards is a man judged before he's had a chance to say his peace and defend himself, does it?"

"What? Are you from Galilee Territory, too?" they lashed back. "Look for yourself. No messenger hails from Galilee, period!"

As the holiday came to a close, everybody went home.

CHAPTER EIGHT

THE 'CATCH-EM-IN-THE-ACT' COMMITTEE

1-11 Everybody except Jesus.

He rode up and spent the night at Olive Mountain. By sunrise, Jesus was at the church-house again. It didn't take long for word to spread that He was there. People flocked to hear Him talk. No sooner than He sat down to start teaching, a ruckus occurred.

The uppity religious types and the Legalists interrupted Jesus by showing off a woman they caught committing unmentionables with a fella that didn't belong to her. They drug her right out in the middle of everybody.

"Teacher," they said to Jesus sarcastic-like, "We found this woman right smack in the middle of her sin with a fella that wasn't hers. In the Bare Standards, ole Moses tells us to chunk stones at her until she's dead. We was just curious what You might have to say." This whole set-up was a trick; they were trying to trap Jesus so they could build a case against Him.

Jesus dropped to a squatting position and started writing something in the dirt with His finger. He didn't answer, but they kept at Him. Finally, He stood up, looked each of the "catch-em-in-the-act-committee" in the eye, and said, "Alright, go ahead. Fire away. But how 'bout this? Why not let the fella among you that has never done a thing wrong be the first to hurl his rock at this woman?"

Jesus dropped back down and kept writing in the dirt. When the "catch-em-in-the-act-committee" heard Jesus's challenge, one by one, you could see rocks falling to the ground. Starting with the oldest, they all emptied their hands and walked away. Now, it was just Jesus and the woman.

When Jesus stood back up, He looked around, and then said to the woman, "Ma'am, where'd they go? There's not a single soul here to condemn you?"

"I reckon not, Lord," she answered.

"Well, it looks like I'm the only One left and I don't condemn you, either," said Jesus. "You're free to go. But you need to change your ways."

12-20 Jesus went back to teaching: "I'm the light for all the world to see. Whoever chooses to follow Me won't have to walk in the dark. He'll have light a-plenty for the rest of his life."

Remembering something Jesus had said earlier, and

trying to catch Him contradicting Himself, the Legalists piped up, “Hey, wait just a doggone minute! You’re tooting your own horn. So—you ‘ain’t worth listening to’.”

“If I carry on about Myself,” Jesus said, “I am still worth listening to because I know where I’m from and where I’m headed. Y’all make your minds up from people logic. I don’t operate that way. And if I make a judgment call, it’s the right call because I ain’t alone in the decision. My Father and I make these calls together.

“And right there in your Book of Standards it says you gotta have two witnesses before something can be proven. Me and My Father got each other’s back on this one.”

They asked Jesus, “Where is Your Father? We don’t see Him! How can we verify anything?”

“Well, I’m standing right here in front of you, and you don’t see Me. Fact is, you don’t know beans about Me or My Father. If you really knew Me, you’d know Him.” This conversation took place in the church office where they kept the offerings and valuables. It wasn’t right out in the middle of the church-house. They could’ve grabbed Him right then, but that wasn’t gonna happen until Jesus decided to let it happen.

21-32 Jesus went back to something He said earlier, “I’ll soon ride off into the sunset; you’ll try to find Me, but in looking for Me, you’ll miss what God really wants you to look for, and you’ll wind up at a dead end, lost in your sin. You can’t follow Me where I’m going.”

The religious types were puzzled, “Is He talking ‘bout

killing himself? Is that what He means by, 'You can't follow Me where I'm going?'"

"You're from down here," Jesus explained, "I'm from up there. This is your home, but not Mine. Yes, I said you'll die in your sins. Dying in your sins is your only option if you choose not to believe who I am."

"Who are you?" they asked point-blank.

"I am who I've been telling you I am since day one," answered Jesus. "I still have a lot to say and a lot of judging to do where you're concerned, but the One that sent Me here is one-hundred percent right, so I just listen to Him and tell you what He says."

They still didn't get that He was talking about God, the Father. So, Jesus kept on explaining, "When I'm hoisted up, you'll know who I am then, and you'll know I wasn't a lone ranger. I'm only saying what My Father taught Me to say. We're always together—My Father and Me. He's never left My side because He's pleased with Me." The more Jesus talked, the more people believed.

Jesus turned to some of the religious types that had changed their minds about Him and started believing in Him, "If you keep going down the trail that My words are leading you down, you'll become a genuine tag-along. You'll eventually reach the truth, and then you'll be set free."

33-41 "But we're kin to ole Abe," they insisted. "We ain't ever been nobody's slave. Why do You think we need setting free?"

“Here’s the deal,” Jesus said. “Once a fella commits a sin, he becomes a slave to sin. A slave is like a drifter because he’s never made to feel that he belongs to a family. But it’s different for a son. He’ll always be kin. So, if the Son in that household cuts the slave loose, then he’s free for sure. I realize you’re kin to ole Abe, but you want to see Me dangling from a tree because you don’t like what I’m saying. But everything I’ve said comes from a front-row seat next to My Father, just like you do what your father taught you to do.”

“Abe’s our father,” they chimed.

“If you were Abe’s kids, you’d do what he did,” said Jesus. “Instead, you want Me dead, and My only crime is telling you the truth as I heard it straight from God. Ole Abe never acted this way. No sir, you learned this by watching your papa.”

They got a bit defensive at that and said, “We’re not half-breeds! We have a legitimate father: the One and Only God.”

42-47 But Jesus didn’t shy away. He drove home His point: “If God was your Father, you couldn’t help but love Me because I came here from Him. I didn’t wander in here on My own. I was sent—by Him! Why are you not getting this through your thick skull? I’ll tell you why. Because you’re deaf to anything I say. Your real papa is the devil, and you’re picking up where he left off. He’s a cold-blooded killer. Always has been. He can’t handle the truth because his whole nature is a lie. He’s a natural-born liar and lying is all he knows because he’s sired every lie that ever crossed a man’s teeth.

No wonder you don't believe Me when I shoot straight with you. How many sins have you seen Me commit? Where's the list? I'm clean and you know it! You also know I'm telling the truth. So why in thunder don't you believe Me?

"Anyone riding with God listens to what God has to say. That's why you're not listening. You're riding for a different brand!"

48-59 The religious types got so mad they went to name-calling, "You ain't nothing but a crazy, demonized Samaritan!"

"I'm not the one with a demon, boys," answered Jesus calmly. "It's the other way around. I choose to bring honor to My Father. You choose to dishonor Me for doing so. I'm not up for no award; not looking for anything for Myself. God is My witness. Know this and know that I mean it: If anyone puts My words into practice, his trail will not end in death—ever!"

The religious folks continued to pick Jesus's words apart, only revealing their ignorance, "You just gave us proof that You're the One with the demon! Ole Abe and all the rest of the old-time messengers all kicked the bucket. But You said, 'If anyone puts My words into practice, his tongue will never taste death—ever!' I don't know what kind o' high horse You're sitting on, Mister, but You ain't better'n our father Abe—God rest his soul—an' Ya ain't better'n none of the old-timers who passed away, either. Just who do You think You are?"

"If I tried to set Myself up on a high horse," answered

Jesus, "I'd get thrown. I'm leaning mightily on My Father. He is the One who has put Me where I truly am—the same God you claim as your own. You think you know Him, but you've never even been close. I know Him. That's just the way it is. I'm not gonna lie and say I don't know Him when I do. That would make Me like you. Truth is, I do know Him, and I hold to His Word. Ole Abe, the one you call your father, was tickled pink to see Me ride off on this journey. He saw this day coming and was slap-happy about it."

Again, the religious folk thought they found more proof that Jesus was crazy, "You ain't even 50-years-old yet, but You've seen ole Abe, have You?"

Jesus leaned in real close to the fella that said that, squared His jaw, and said, "I can say this without batting an eye: Before Abe ever was, I am."

When Jesus said that, they went to picking up as may stones as they could, as fast as they could. They'd had enough. It was time to give Him "what-for!" But when they looked up to aim, He was gone! They checked the whole church-house, but it was like He disappeared.

CHAPTER NINE

FROM CAN'T SEE TO CAN SEE

1-7 Jesus and His tag-alongs saw a man who'd been blind all his life. They asked Jesus, "Who's fault is it that this fella is blind? Is he paying for something he did or something his parents did?"

"Wrong on both counts," answered Jesus. "This is not about finding someone to blame. It's about seeing an opportunity to let God work in his life. We need to take advantage of every opportunity to do God's work while it's still daylight. No sense in putting it off 'til dark when nobody can see it. While I'm here, I'm the light of the world."

Jesus spit. His spit hit the dirt. He bent down and started rolling His spit in the dirt with His fingers. The tag-alongs just sort o' looked at each other and shrugged: "Jesus was making mud-pies?" they thought to themselves. He took the mud-pie and smeared it on the blind fella's eyes.

The man didn't know what was happening, but he listened to Jesus's instructions: "Walk over to Siloam's pond just yonder and wash this gook off your eyes." The blind fella did just what Jesus told him to do and when he came back, he could see!

8-12 Blind no more, he walked all over town with a big ole grin on his face. He didn't recognize anybody, but they sure recognized him, "Hey, ain't that the blind fella that's always begging off us?" Others agreed, "Yep. That's him." But others argued, "Naw, that ain't him. But they do sort o' look alike."

"It is me! I am the fella y'all are talking about!" he answered.

Nearly every one of them waved their hands in front of the fella's face with their mouths dropped open and asked, "How is it possible for you to be able to see, all o' sudden-like?"

He told them how it happened, "Some fellas with Jesus started asking questions about me. Jesus stopped, made a mud-pie, and . . . "

"Now, wait just a dog-gone minute," one of the neighbors interrupted. "He did what?"

"He made a mud-pie," he continued. "Then He smeared it on my eyes and sent me to the pond to wash it off. When I started a-washin,' I started a-seein'!"

"Where'd He go?" they asked.

"Beats me," the seeing man shrugged.

13-17 The seeing man's neighbors couldn't leave well enough alone, so they drug him over to let the Legalists have a look at him. Care to guess what day it was that this all happened? You got it! It was a holy day. So, the Legalists made the seeing man repeat his story.

"Like I said, He smeared mud on my eyes and told me to wash," he told them. "As soon as I washed, I could see."

Some of the Legalists crossed their arms, huffed, and said, "It's obvious this Jesus Fella ain't from God because He don't carry an ounce of concern for the holy day!" But others were a little more honest in trying to figure things out and asked, "But how can a bad guy do good things that require such power?" The Legalists couldn't agree.

They turned to the seeing man and asked his opinion of Jesus, "What do you think of this Fella that gave you seeing eyes?"

"No doubt in my mind, He ain't from around here. He's a messenger from up yonder," he answered.

18-22 Well, the religious folks weren't buying this story. They were dismissing it as a hoax until they visited with the seeing man's folks.

"Now be honest with us," they said. "Is this your boy that you said was born blind? Can you folks explain to us how come he can see now?"

"Of course, he's our boy." the parents answered. "Yes, he's been blind all his life—up 'til now. We don't have a clue how he can see now or who done it. He may have been blind, but he ain't dumb. Why don't you ask him? He's old enough to speak for himself."

The seeing man's parents skirted the issue about Jesus because they knew if anyone was caught saying Jesus was the Promised One, the religious folk would remove their names from the church-house roll and wouldn't be allowed inside. That's why they said, "He's old enough to speak for himself."

24-34 So, they brought the seeing man back in for a second round of interrogating, "Come clean before God. We know this Man is an evil sinner!"

"That may be! I don't know," replied the seeing man. "All's I know is: I ain't blind no more. I went from 'can't see' to 'can see'!"

They asked him again, gritting their teeth, "What did He do to you? How exactly did He get your eyes to open?"

The seeing man was getting flustered, "I already done told you. I may have been the one that was blind, but y'all got a hearin' problem! Or maybe y'all just enjoy hearin' me tell it over and over. Is that it? Y'all act like you're anxious to become one o' His tag-alongs."

The religious types lost their religion and let the insults fly, "You're His tag-along! Not us! We follow ole Moses (God rest his soul). We know God and Moses were partners, but this Jesus Fella—He just showed up outta nowhere!"

"Ain't this somethin'?" said the seeing man. "He gives eyesight to a blind man and y'all think He just showed up outta nowhere. Think about it. God don't listen to evil sinners.

God listens to the God-fearing types—those that do what He wants ‘em to do. There ain't never been a time where a man opened the eyes of another man who was born blind. If this Fella weren't from God, He couldn't do stuff like that."

The religious types got all uppity (and, in fact, returned to the discussion that started the whole thing, when Jesus's tag-alongs asked if the blind man was paying for something he or his parents had done), "You ain't nothing but a filthy sinner your whole life! Who are you to think you can start lecturing us?" They tossed the seeing man out.

35-41 When Jesus got wind that the seeing man had been tossed out, He went looking for him, found him, and asked, "Do you believe in the Son of Man?"

"I'd like to, Mister. Who is He?" the seeing man asked.

Jesus smiled and chuckled, "You're looking at Him and talking to Him."

The seeing man dropped to his knees in front of Jesus, and said, "I believe with all my heart, Lord."

Jesus explained, "I came here to set things in order—stir things up a bit. I'm gonna open the eyes of those who couldn't see and shut the eyes of the ones who can see, but refuse to see the truth."

Some of the Legalists were eavesdropping and asked, "So now, You're saying we're the blind ones?"

Jesus answered, "If you truly were blind and owned up to it, your sin would go away. But because you think you can see everything so perfectly well, your sin stays put."

CHAPTER TEN

THE MASTER HORSEMAN

1-5 "Here's the simple truth: If a fella don't use the gate, but climbs over the fence where you keep your horses, that fella's planning to steal you blind. The owner of the horses uses the front gate. He can go in any time he wants because they're his stock. The hired hand will even open the gate for him. Fact is, a horse knows her owner's voice. He can call her by name and she'll head toward him. He can go for a walk and his horse will tag right along behind him. A horse won't act the same way for a stranger. She'll be skittish around someone she don't know."

6-18 Jesus was trying to teach them something, but they weren't getting it. So, He tried to help them understand, "Think of Me as the Fella who opens the gate. Other folk have tried to steal the horses, but the horses wouldn't cooperate. I'm at the gate. Horses going in and out through Me will be in good hands and enjoy wide-open pastures. A horse thief has only evil in mind. He wants to take, kill, or tear up. The reason I came here was to make sure them horses could have the best life possible.

"I'm the Master Horseman. I'll give My life for the horses. The hired hand, since he don't own the horses or have much invested in them, will run off and leave the horses at the first sign of trouble. That won't be good for the horses. But that's what happens with someone who don't care much about the horses.

"I'm the Master Horseman. I know My own horses well, and they know Me, just like the Father and I know each other. He also knows I intend to give My life for those horses. I've got some more horses from a different line that I'll bring along, also. They'll come running when I call and join in with the rest of My horses. Then it'll be just us.

"My Father knows that I'll lay My life down and rise back up, and He loves Me for it. Nobody's gonna take My life. I'm gonna die willingly. I can do that. I can lay it down, and I can bring it back up. This is what My Father wants Me to do."

19-21 The more Jesus talked, the greater the split grew among the religious folks. Most of them just thought He was crazy or had a demon inside Him, "Why do y'all even listen to Him?"

Others said, "Demons don't talk like that, and they sure as heck don't open up blind eyes!"

After adding a few sticks to the fire, Thunder Johnson studied your faces. It's like he was seeing right through you. He knew what you and the others were thinking. Some of you were fighting the same battle as the crowd in the story, trying to figure out if Jesus was from above or below. If Jesus really did all those miracles, it meant He had power no one else had. Thunder spoke to the group along those lines, reminding them of what Jesus said. "He was guilty of no sin. He was only guilty of helping people, healing people, and talking about God in a more personal way than anyone else ever had." Thunder lowered his head and swung it slowly back and forth. Then said, "I sure never knew God before like I did after I started down the trail with Jesus."

Thunder chuckled at himself and said, "Let me get back to telling the story."

22-33 It was winter time and there was another shin-dig in Jerusalem. Jesus was strolling up to the church-house and got just up to the front steps when the religious folk penned Him up in a circle and wanted answers, "How long are You gonna keep up all this guesswork? Tell us right now—no beating around the bush: Are You or are You not the Promised One?"

Jesus shook His head, "I've been telling you, but it hadn't clicked. You've seen the miracles and you've heard Me give credit to My Father. That ought to be enough. Far from it. The reason you don't believe in Me has to do with what's branded on your flanks. Check it and see: You don't belong to Me. You're a stray. My horses recognize My voice when they hear it, and they nuzzle right up to Me. They're gonna live forever, and won't be put down—ever! This is what I give them. Nobody is gonna take them away from Me. No one comes close to sizing up with My Father who gave them to Me. If you think anyone is powerful enough to wrestle them out of My Father's hands, you're seriously mistaken. The two of us are hitched up tighter 'n two pregnant mules."

There they went again, fumbling around on the ground for some rocks to chunk at Jesus.

While the religious folks were loading themselves down with ammunition, Jesus spoke, "I've done a lot of good things that helped others with My Father's help. Just exactly which one of those good things causes you to want Me dead?"

"We ain't after Your hide for no good works," they answered. "But we can't tolerate a man trying to make himself out to be God. That's pure blasphemy!"

34-39 Jesus had a little fun with them. Since they seemed to like setting traps for Him, He returned the favor when He asked, "In your Good Book, doesn't God say, 'I tell you that y'all are gods'? (Quote from Psalm 82:6) If God called your kinfolk 'gods'—and you know the Bible don't fib, why are you all out o' sorts with Me, calling Me a blasphemer just 'cause I said, 'I'm the Son of God'? My Father sent Me here to tell you that. If the proof ain't in the pudding, don't believe Me! But if I am doing My Father's works and you refuse to believe Me, take your eyes off of Me for a spell and ponder a bit closer on the works themselves. Then maybe you can add two and two together and finally get you an 'A-ha!' moment where you plainly see what's right in front of you—the inseparable relationship My Father and I have with each other."

They tried again to jump Him, but when the dust settled, He was nowhere in the scuffle pile.

40-42 Jesus revisited the place where He saw ole Johnnie baptizing folks on the other side of the Jordan River, and He camped there for a bit. Lots of folks gathered near Jesus and talked amongst themselves, "I don't recall Johnnie ever doing any miracles, but he sure spoke the truth about this Fella." And right there in the same place that Johnnie started telling people about Jesus a couple of years earlier, a whole bunch of folks put their trust in Jesus.

CHAPTER ELEVEN

MOVE THAT STONE

1-3 A fella by the name of Lazarus who lived in Bethany took on an illness. Lazarus had a couple of sisters, Mary and Martha. It was this same Mary that would later scrub Jesus's feet with some store-bought smell-good stuff and dry His feet, using her hair as a towel. Jesus got word from Lazarus's sisters that His good friend was in bad shape.

4-9 Jesus said, "This sickness Lazarus has contracted won't do him in. It came along for a reason. God's got something special planned that'll cause folk to sit up and take notice of the Son of God." Jesus loved that whole family deeply. But He didn't leave to go check on Lazarus right away. He just piddled around a couple of days. Finally, Jesus said, "Let's take a ride back to Judea."

"You think that's wise, Sir?" His tag-alongs were glad to

be away from folks who always seemed to want to chunk rocks at them. “Why climb back into a den of rattlers?”

“There’s twelve hours of daylight, give or take an hour,” Jesus answered. “It’s easier to see where you’re going during the daylight hours, thanks to the light of the world. It ain’t so easy walking at night though. A fella’s liable to trip over himself because he’s got no light.”

11-16 Jesus sighed for a moment, and then continued, “Our buddy Lazarus has dozed off. I need to go wake him up.”

But the tag-alongs drew on their vast medical knowledge and said, “Whoa, Boss! Sleeping’s good for a sick fella.”

Jesus was using the idea of “sleep” to mean that he was dead. But they didn’t know that was how He meant it. So, Jesus spelled it out, “Lazarus is dead. It’s worked out for the best that I wasn’t there when he died. Up to now, the fire of your faith has been kindled with a few small sticks and limbs. I think it’s about time we threw a great big ole log on that fire. Let’s ride!”

Tommy, one of the tag-alongs who went by the nickname, “Twin,” saw the hesitation in their eyes. They weren’t sure about riding back into certain death. But Twin spurred his horse and said, “Come on! If they kill Him, we might as well die by His side!”

17-20 As Jesus rode into the village, He learned that Lazarus had been buried for four days. They didn’t stick their dead in the ground in that part of the world. They wrapped them up and put them in caves they called "tombs." Bethany, Lazarus's hometown, was only about two miles from Jerusalem. There were a lot of religious folks who came out to help Mary and Martha grieve over their dead brother. Martha got word that Jesus was coming, and she jumped up and ran to meet Him. But Mary didn't leave the house.

21-27 Martha unloaded her grief on Jesus, "Lord, if only You could o' been here, he wouldn't o' died. Even so, it's plain to me that You could ask God to do anything, and He'd do it."

"Your brother's fixing to get back up," Jesus told Martha.

"I know he will, Lord," she agreed. "He'll get back up on that day to end all days."

Jesus said, "I'm the One who brings folks back from the dead and gives them life. When a fella believes in Me, even when death tries to take him, he'll keep living. If you're Mine, you don't die—ever!" Jesus looked right into Martha's eyes and asked, "Do you understand what I'm saying?"

"Yes, Lord," she answered, "I'm a firm believer that You're the Promised One, the Son of God, who came here for us."

28-32 Martha turned and went back into the house. She whispered to Mary, her sister, "Jesus is here and He wants to see you." Mary darted out of the house and went to Jesus. Jesus hadn't made His presence known to everybody. He wasn't in town. He was still where Martha found Him. The religious folk that had been helping the sisters grieve saw Mary run outside, so they followed her, thinking she was headed back to cry at her brother's tomb.

When Mary found Jesus, she dropped to the ground in front of Him, and repeated the words of her sister, "Lord, if only You could o' been here, he wouldn't o' died!"

33-43 This was the closest Jesus had ever been to death and He didn't like it. He watched Mary cry. He saw the religious folk crying. A holy anger spun like a tornado inside His Spirit, and He was filled with raw emotion.

"Show Me where you put him," Jesus said.

"This way," they said as they led Jesus to the tomb.

Jesus's heart spilt over with tears, and He wept.

The religious folk saw it and said, "He really loved him!"

Others said, "But how could He be there to help a blind man that He didn't know, and not be here to keep a friend from dying?"

Jesus was still driven by a holy anger when He approached the tomb. There was a stone covering the entrance to the cave where Lazarus was buried.

"Move that stone," Jesus said. Martha didn't think that was a very good idea. She warned Jesus, "Lord, he's been dead four days. It's gonna smell somethin' fierce."

Jesus turned to Martha and said, "Didn't I tell you that this trail of faith you're on leads to the incredible sight of God's glory?"

Martha nodded and they moved the stone. Jesus looked

up and prayed, "Father, thanks for listening. You're always listening, but these folks don't know that. So, I'm talking to You out loud to give them a chance to believe that You sent Me."

Jesus then stood tall and hollered with a loud voice, *"Lazarus, come here!"* A dead man came out of the tomb still wrapped up in grave clothes from head to toe. Jesus said, "Get him out of them dead man's clothes and help him back into his jeans 'n boots!"

45-53 A living, walking, talking Lazarus was more than enough to convince a bunch more religious types to believe in Jesus. But it terrified some of them, and they rode back to the Legalists and told what Jesus did.

So, the uppity religious types and the Legalists held a meeting with all the religious big-wigs assembled together. "We gotta do something," one of them said, "This Jesus Fella has stepped it up a notch. If we don't stop Him, it won't be long before the whole country believes in Him. If that happens, I guarantee you the Roman government will clear us out of leadership and wipe out our country!"

Caiaphas, the biggest big-wig of them all, rebuked the fella that just spoke, "You don't know a piddling thing! Clearly, the best thing that can happen is for one fella to die for everybody else instead of letting the whole country go under."

Ole Caiaphas was a messenger of God without even knowing it. It's like God had ahold of his tongue and was announcing ahead o' time that Jesus was gonna die for the nation. But His death wouldn't touch just that one country; it would bind all of God's children together from all over the world.

Starting that day, they set out a plan to kill Jesus. Jesus avoided any contact with the religious folk, and headed out to the desert. He and his tag-alongs holed up in a little place called Ephraim.

55-57 The time for the Annual Rodeo came around again, and the crowds started gathering in Jerusalem from all around, getting themselves ready. They all had their eyes peeled for any sign of Jesus. Talk around the church-house was constant, "Do you think He'll show up?"

The uppity religious types and the Legalists had "Wanted" posters all over the place. A warrant had been issued for His arrest.

CHAPTER TWELVE

THE CURE FOR WHAT MAKES THE WORLD SICK

1-8 Six days before the Annual Rodeo's Big Dinner, Jesus paid a visit to Lazarus in Bethany. They were still celebrating what Jesus did for them and they wanted to fix a special supper for Jesus to show their appreciation. Martha was fixing and serving like usual. Lazarus was enjoying Jesus's company at the supper table. Mary had thought long and hard about how she could show Jesus what He meant to her and her kin. She took some high dollar, store-bought smell-good stuff and poured it over Jesus's feet. She tenderly rubbed and scrubbed His feet with it, and then dried His feet with her hair. The whole house smelt like that stuff.

One of the tag-alongs, Judas Iscariot (who was fixing to

turn Jesus in for a reward) said, "That was some high-dollar stuff, and she just wasted it. She coulda sold it for a hefty sum and given it to poor folks." The "poor folks" were the last thing on his thieving mind. He was in charge of their cash pot and wasn't against helping himself to some of it every once in a while.

Jesus answered, "Mind your own business. She's been saving this up for this occasion, to use it in anticipation of My burial. You'll have poor folk around you for the rest of your life. But I won't be around much longer."

9-11 Somehow, Jesus's whereabouts became known to a large group of religious folk. They wanted to see Jesus and to see the living version of a man once dead—Lazarus. The jealousy of the uppity religious types had risen to the point that they wanted Lazarus dead, too—again! Lazarus was the cause of a whole bunch of folks abandoning their religion and believing in Jesus.

12-14 The next day, rumor spread like wildfire that Jesus was on His way to Jerusalem. They cut down willow branches and ran out to meet Him when they saw Him come riding in. They were shouting: "Hooray! Give honor to Him who rides with God—the King of Israel!" (Quote from Psalm 118:26)

Jesus rode into Jerusalem on the back of a colt donkey, just like it was predicted in the Good Book: "There's nothing to be afraid of, young-un of Zion (that's the Good Book's name for Jerusalem): Look yonder! Your King's heading this way riding a donkey's colt." (Quote from Zechariah 9:9)

16-19 At this point, Jesus's tag-alongs were pretty much clueless about what was going on. But after it was all over with, they remembered how all this happened and found how it all fit in with the Good Book. Word kept spreading about how Jesus called Lazarus back from the dead. Those who saw it happen couldn't stop talking about it. Their enthusiasm over this miracle spread through the whole town and was the reason so many folks were there to greet Him when He arrived.

It was more than the Legalists could stomach. None of their threats were paying off. They were even starting to turn on each other, "Do you see this? We ain't gained one inch of ground! Look at this: He's got the whole world tagging along behind Him!"

20-33 Some of the folk that came to Jerusalem for the festivities were from the country of Greece. They approached Phil—probably because he was an outsider, too (since he was from Galilee Territory)—and said, "Mister, we wanna see Jesus."

Phil told Andy about their request; then Andy and Phil went and told Jesus. Jesus was staring down, but not really looking at anything in particular. For a long time, He said nothing. Then He let out a long breath, and said, "It's time."

He looked up at Andy and Phil to explain what He meant, "Pay attention to what I'm about to say: What good is a grain of wheat if it just sits there all by its lonesome? It'll never be more than just a single grain. But if that grain of wheat lands in the dirt and dies, it'll bring to life a big ole crop of wheat.

"Whoever tries to hold onto life real tight ends up losing it, but whoever's ready to trade in the life this world has to offer gets a better deal—a forever life! If you want to help Me, you must follow Me. Don't matter where I go, My helpers are gonna be by My side. Anybody that helps Me is gonna be well taken care of by My Father.

"My insides are all knotted up, but what can I do? I can't hardly ask to sit this one out when this is what I came for. Father, this is for You. I hope I do You proud."

Suddenly, a Heaven Voice spoke back to Jesus: "I'm already proud of You, Son. And You are going to make Me proud again."

People all around there heard the Heaven Voice and figured it was thunder. Others shook their heads and said, "No, an angel just talked to Jesus!"

Jesus addressed their concerns, "The Heaven Voice was not for Me. It was for your benefit. You needed to hear that voice because you need to know that the issues of this world are about to be settled. And the evil one that's been running the show is about to get booted off stage. I expect I'll soon be hanging high off the ground. But from there, I'll be able to wrap My arms around the whole world and draw every last one of you to Me." Jesus was actually telling them how He was going to die before it happened.

34-36 His words confused the crowd. They asked Him a fair question, "Doesn't the Good Book say that the Promised One will stick around for good? So, what are You meaning when You say, 'I'll soon be hanging high off the ground?' Are You the Promised One or someone else?"

Jesus didn't give them a "yes" or "no" answer. He said, "The light will only be around a little bit longer. Take advantage of the light. Get done what you need done while you still have it. Darkness will soon be here and you don't want to get stuck in the dark. You don't know which way to turn when its pitch black all around you. Right now, you have the light. Now's a good time to believe in the light, so you can forever belong to the light." Jesus backed away as He spoke these words; then He went into hiding again.

37-41 Even after all the things He'd done, they really didn't have a life-changing faith in Him. But the Good Book already knew that would happen. Ole Isaiah wrote, "Lord, has anyone believed our story? Has anyone seen Your extended arm?" (Quote from Isaiah 53:1) That's why they couldn't get it. Isaiah also wrote, "He's blindfolded their eyes and turned their hearts stone cold, to keep them from seeing or understanding, and be changed so I could heal them." (Quote from Isaiah 6:10) Isaiah wrote this after he'd been allowed to see God's waterfall-like glory poured into Jesus.

42-43 Having said all that, the head count for those that did believe in Jesus was nothing to snort at. Even some of the uppity folk, both religious and political, were convinced that Jesus was the Promised One. They didn't come right out and fess up because they didn't want to get kicked out of the church-house. Seems like a constant and universal problem among believers: Always struggling with wanting to be a man-pleaser instead of a God-pleaser.

44-50 Jesus spoke again with a loud voice, "You put your faith in Me, but more than just Me; it's also in the One who sent Me here. And if you're looking at Me, you might as well be looking at Him. I'm here to bring light to a dark world, and if you'll believe in Me, you'll be rid of your darkness.

"If a fella tosses My words aside, I'll not sentence or condemn him. I'm not here to inspect the world's diseases; I'm here to provide the cure for what makes the world sick. The fella that rejects Me and My words will see those words return as his judge at the last round. I'm only saying what My Father who sent Me has told Me to say. I'm following His direct order. It's a matter of eternal life and death, so I'm careful to tell you word for word what My Father told Me."

CHAPTER THIRTEEN

SCRUB ME GOOD ALL OVER

1-5 Just before the Annual Rodeo's Meaningful Meal of Memories, Jesus knew it was time for Him to do what He came to do and ride beyond the sunsets of this world to return to His Father. But Jesus had fallen in love with all those in the world who had chosen to ride with His Father's brand. Now that the end was in sight, Jesus's love for them was even stronger.

By the time supper came around, Judas had already danced with the devil, and his heart was all set to betray Jesus. Jesus kept the big picture in mind: His Father had placed the whole plan to save the world into Jesus's hands, and Jesus would soon return to His Father who sent Him. So, Jesus got up from the supper table, took off His leather vest, and tied a towel to His belt loop. Then, He poured water into a small wash tub and commenced removing His tag-alongs' boots, washing their stinky ole feet, and drying them off with the towel that hung from His belt loop.

6-11 When He sidled up to Rocky to pull his boots off, Rocky asked, "Lord, what are You doing?"

Jesus answered him, "I know you don't understand it now, but trust Me when I tell you that it'll all make sense later on."

Rocky shook his head, "I can't! I can't let You do it!"

"If I don't," Jesus warned, "it means you aren't one of Mine."

Rocky started tugging at his clothes, "In that case, Lord, scrub me good all over!"

"Hold on!" Jesus stopped him. "You had a bath! You're all clean except your nasty ole feet." Jesus repeated Himself as He looked first at Rocky, and then the rest of them, "You're clean . . . but not all of you." Jesus intended that last part for the one He knew would hand Him over for a profit. I reckon that stung a bit.

12-15 When Jesus was done washing their feet and put His vest back on, He laid back in a reclining position and asked, "Anybody know why I just did that? Y'all look at Me as your Teacher and Boss. And rightly so. Since your Boss and Teacher has bent down to help you by washing your stinking feet, y'all ought to do the same for each other. I've set an example for you to follow, and I expect you to do for each other what I done for you.

16-20 "See here: A hired hand is not better than his foreman, and an errand boy is not better than the fella he's running those errands for. Knowing this stuff is one thing. Doing it is where you find the reward. I'm not talking about every one of you; I know who I've chosen just like I know who's been making deals with the devil. It's all in the Good Book: 'The fella that ate from My own table is gunning for Me.' (Quote from Psalm 41:9)

"I'm letting y'all know about it now, so it won't catch you by surprise, and it'll deepen your trust in Me. Just so you'll know: There's a chain reaction—a connection. When a fella welcomes someone that I sent to him, that fella is welcoming Me, and when he welcomes Me, he welcomes the One who sent Me."

21-30 Something had been troubling Jesus for quite some time, and it kept growing inside Him. Finally, He blurted it out, "One of you is gonna turn Me in!"

They all got bug-eyed, looking around the table at each other—wondering who the traitor was. One of the tag-alongs that felt a kinship to Jesus was sitting right next to Him. Rocky gave him a nod, wanting him to dig some more out of Jesus so they could find the rascal. So, he leaned over to Jesus, and sort of whispered to Him, "Boss, who is it?"

Jesus whispered back, "He's the one I'm fixing to give this piece of bread to after I sop it." When Jesus sopped His bread, He handed it to Judas, Simon Iscariot's boy. That piece of bread went down Judas's throat hard. Judas looked at Jesus with the eyes of the devil. Jesus looked at Judas and said, "Whatever you're gonna do, get it over with!"

Nobody else knew what was going on or why Jesus said that to Judas. They just figured Jesus was sending him out with a shopping list or some poor folks to give money to since Judas held the money pot. Judas stepped out into the darkness, still trying to swallow that last bite.

31-38 Once Judas was gone, Jesus told the rest, "Now, the ball is rolling and I'm going to show what I'm made of, which will also show what God is made of. God and I are going to work together quickly, so pay attention. You don't want to miss what you are about to learn as you watch God work through Me.

"Boys, we don't have much time with each other. I trust you'll come looking for Me, but it's like I told the religious folk, 'You can't get where I'm going,' so now I'm telling you the same.

"Let Me give you one final, but very important message: I insist that you love each other. The same way I've loved you—you ought to love each other just like it. This is how folk will know that you are My tag-alongs, if you're not ashamed to love each other."

Rocky was blunt and asked, "Boss, where are you headed?"

Jesus held Rocky by the shoulders and said, "Even if I told you, the trail would end before you found Me. But you'll pick the trail up again when it's your time."

Rocky had another question, “Boss, how ‘bout I just stick right by Your side? I’ll take a bullet for You!”

“Is that so?” Jesus asked. “You’d take a bullet for Me? You’d give your life for Mine? I know you mean well, but the fact is: Before the next crow of the rooster, you’ll deny Me three times.”

CHAPTER FOURTEEN

NO OTHER TRAIL

1-6 "Don't fret. It's not a time for your heart to fill up with fear. It's time for faith. God fetched you this far—trust Him! And while you're at it, trust Me. Let Me tell you about My Father's place. He's got a big ole house—bigger'n any mansion you could wrap your mind around. There's room a' plenty for you to make yourself at home. If none of this was true, why would I waste time making it up? I'm headed there to make room for you. When everything is good and ready, I'll be back to get you, so we can all be together again. Deep down inside, you already know the trail I'm taking."

Tommy said, "Boss, I don't have a clue where You're headed. How do You expect us to pick up Your trail?"

Jesus said, "I'm the trail; and as you go down that trail, you'll also find that I'm the truth; and the longer you're on that trail, the more you'll realize the trail never ends. That's when you'll understand that I'm also the life. No other trail leads to the Father. The only way is through Me.

7-11 "Know Me, and you'll know My Father. Fact is, you already know Him. You've even seen Him."

"Could You show us the Father, Boss?" asked Phil. "That'd be plenty enough for us."

"You mean to tell Me, you've been riding with Me all this time, Phil, and you never once took a look at Me?" Jesus stood face to face with Phil and said, "Look at Me." Phil looked into Jesus's eyes and Jesus said, "Alright, now you've seen the Father.

"How can you stand there and ask Me to show you the Father? Haven't you been listening? Don't you believe Me when I tell you that I'm in the Father and the Father's in Me? I open My mouth, but it's His words that come out. I reach My hand out to touch someone, but it's My Father's fingertips that they feel. Put every ounce of your faith in this: I am in Him and He is in Me. If that's too much for you, let the works themselves convince you.

12-18 "Here's something else for you to chew on: The fella that believes in Me can do the same stuff I do. Heck, he can even outdo the stuff I've done, because I'm joining back up with the Father. You can ask for anything in My name, an' I'll do it, because I know it'll bring glory to My Father. I'm not blowing smoke. I'll do anything you ask Me to do when you call out to Me.

"You want to show Me that you love Me? Do what I've told you to do. I'm going to ask My Father (and I know He'll do it) to give you another Partner just like Me to be by your side always. He is the Heaven-Sent Spirit of Truth. Now, this "eyes-and-ears" world won't even notice Him. But you'll know Him, because you'll feel Him—not just around you, but inside you. I can't bear the thought of leaving you like a bunch of orphans; I'll be on My way back as soon as possible."

19-24 "It won't be much longer and folks won't be able to see Me anymore. But you'll see Me. You're gonna be alive in a way you've never been alive before because you're gonna experience life through Me. Right then and there, you'll have a settled confidence in your soul, knowing that I am in My Father, you're in Me, and I'm in you. Never giving up on what I tell you to do is evidence of your love for Me. My Father loves those that love Me. You'll get My love in return, and a bunch more. Your understanding of Me will grow, more and more."

Another tag-along with the same name as the traitor, Judas, said to Jesus, "How is it that we're gonna be able to see You, but no one else can?"

"Here's how it works," Jesus answered. "You keep loving Me and keep true to My words. My Father will love you like His own, and We will come to you and live inside you. If you don't keep true to My words, then you really don't love Me. I can't tell you how important My words are! They're not just My words. They come straight from the Father who sent Me to you.

25-31 "I'm doing My best to tell you all I can while I'm physically in front of you. But your soon-to-be Partner, the Holy Spirit, the One I'm gonna have the Father send to you, will teach you everything you need to know and help you recall all the stuff I told you about.

"If I could reach into My saddle bags and give each of you a gift, it would be exactly what I'm about to give you, only it don't come wrapped in a purty box: PEACE. I leave you with the gift of My peace. My gift-giving ain't the same as the world's. This is something you need to keep your heart from getting all tied up in knots and to keep going without being afraid of nothing.

"I've said it already and you heard Me, 'I'm leaving and I'm coming back.' Step outside your own feelings for a moment and be happy for Me that I'm headed back to My Father, the greatest of all. You can do this because you love Me. I'm telling y'all this stuff now, so that when it happens, it'll deepen your faith in Me.

"There's not much time left for Me to tell you a whole lot more. The devil's coming after Me. His posse is almost here." Jesus smirked at the thought of the devil coming to take Him with great force and power, knowing that His power was much greater than the devil's. He said, "He's got nothing on Me. In fact, His weakness will bring Me closer to My purpose. I'm gonna get to show the world just how much I love My Father. I'm gonna see My Father's plans all the way through.

"Let's get out of here."

CHAPTER FIFTEEN

WAGON LOADS OF FRUIT

1-8 Jesus and His tag-alongs came upon some grape vines, and Jesus turned the vineyard into an outdoor classroom: "I am the Genuine Vine and My Father tends to the Vine. He pays attention to every little branch and shoot. If one of them is shy of fruit, He cuts it off. He trims the ones that make fruit, so they can make more next time. You've already been trimmed by listening to My words. Stay attached to Me, and I'll hold onto you. You can do nothing without Me, no more than a branch can make fruit on its own.

"I'm the Vine; you're branches. Are you with Me?" Jesus asked. They nodded, sort of slow-like, so He kept on: "If we stay together—you and Me—your life will amount to something. In other words, you'll make a big ole bunch of grapes that'll make My Father smile. But none of this will happen if you aren't sticking right next to Me. If you pull away from Me, you won't be worth nothing. You'll be like a branch that broke itself off from the vine. After it dries up and gets all withered-like, it'll be thrown into the burn pile. If you stick close to Me and My words stay in your heart, you can ask for anything, and it'll be done for you. This is how My Father enjoys Himself: seeing y'all bringing in wagon loads of fruit because it proves to Him that you're tagging-along close to Me.

9-17 "I've loved you with the same love the Father has for Me. Sit as tight in that love as you would in your saddle should your horse try to toss you. The way to do that is to keep doing what I told you to do. That's how I stay so close to My Father.

"I'm telling you these things because I want you to have My joy inside you—real joy! Joy that fills you up so much, it starts spilling over. I'm not asking you; I'm telling you: Love each other with the same love I've showed you. The greatest love there is, is when a fella is willing to die for his partners. You're My partners, and you prove it when you mind what I say. I don't consider you hirelings, because a hireling don't know what his foreman has planned. That's why you're My partners, because I've held nothing back from you. You've heard every word My Father has said to Me. You really didn't join up with Me on your own. I picked you out. I had a plan in mind for you all along—a plan that'll bear fruit forever. So, you can go ahead and ask the Father anything you want where I'm concerned, and He'll make it happen. In case you didn't get it the first time or the second time, I'm gonna tell you again: Love each other!

18-25 "If the world don't like you, don't take it personal-like. They hated Me first, so naturally they're gonna hate you. If you weren't any different from them, they'd love you like kinfolk! But you ain't like them anymore. I plucked you out from among them. That's the real reason they hate you. You know, I said: 'A hireling is no better than his foreman.' If they're gonna draw down on Me, they're gonna draw down on you. But if they cottoned to what I had to say, they'll listen to you, too. The way everybody treats you is on account of who I am, because they don't know the One who's behind it all. I stirred up the hornet's nest. I came along and pointed out their faults and ruined their ignorance and contentment. As far as they knew, they didn't have no faults. Now, they don't have a leg to stand on if they try to plead ignorance. They can hate Me for it, but they'll be hating My Father at the same time. I showed them stains on their souls that they didn't think was there. No one ever done that before. They could've acted as if they were perfect had I not come along and pointed at their stains. But how could I let that happen? Now they've seen the truth and reality of both Me and My Father, and they've chosen to hate Us both. But this, too, is in the Good Book: 'They hated Me for nothing.' (Quote from Psalm 69:4)

26-27 "When the Partner gets here, the One I told you about (the Spirit of Truth) that I'll send your way when I am with the Father– He's gonna support and affirm all that I am. You're gonna do the same, because you've rode with Me from the very start."

CHAPTER SIXTEEN

HANG ONTO YOUR SADDLES!

1-4 "By telling y'all these things, I'm trying to prepare y'all for when you hit some rough terrain. Y'all can expect to be kicked out of the church-houses. But that's the least of your worries. Y'all need to know that it'll eventually get so bad, folk will think they'd be doing God a favor by killing you. Just remember, they act like this cause they don't know Me or My Father. I'm just warning you that it will happen. I didn't tell you this earlier, on account of I was here with you.

5-11 "But now I'm going away to the One who sent Me here. You've stopped asking Me, 'Where are you headed?' You're just sitting there moping like someone stole your girl. I know it hurts to hear Me talk like this. But I have to be up front with you. It's best for you that I leave. If I don't, your

Partner won't come. When I leave, I'll send Him directly. When He gets here, He'll have three main jobs: He'll show folks the error of their ways, He'll point them in the direction of right living, and He'll warn them that they'll be accountable for what they do with their lives. The biggest fault that He'll show them is their failure to believe in Me. He'll also be needed to teach folk about right living, because I won't be around down here. And He'll warn them 'bout being accountable, on account of the top dog of this world, the devil, is already getting his come-up-ins.

12-15 "There's so much more I could tell y'all, but I think you're about to bust as it is. When the Spirit of Truth gets here, He'll guide you down the trail of truth. He won't lead you astray because He only repeats what He hears. And He's gonna let y'all know what's heading your way. He'll be true to Me and stick with what I tell Him to tell you. I'm sitting on Heaven's treasure box. Every bit of what the Father has also belongs to Me. That's why I can give it to Him to give to you.

16-19 "You won't see Me for a while, but then after a while, you'll see Me again."

Some of the tag-alongs had to rumble that one around in their minds for a bit. They asked each other what Jesus meant by, "You won't see Me for a while, but then after a while, you'll see Me again," and "I'm headed to My Father." They said, "What the heck is He talking about? What does 'a little while' mean?"

Jesus watched them jaw back and forth and knew they had questions, so He said, "Let me guess: Y'all want to know what I meant when I said, 'You won't see Me for a while, but then after a while, you'll see Me again'?

20-24 "Let Me throw some more at you: While y'all cry and mourn, everybody else will be celebrating. But your sadness will eventually turn itself upside down with joy. When a woman's having a baby, you can hear her screaming for miles, cause child-bearing is painful. But once the baby is born, the woman's screams turn to smiles; her pain brought pleasure since she realizes she's added a new face to the world. It's the same with you: It hurts now. But I'll be back. And your heart will dance to a tune of joy that no one can take away. I'm looking forward to that day, too, so I won't have to answer so many cotton-picking questions!

"Seriously, though: Ask all you want. Not just questions—needs, too. And when you ask for something and My Father can see Me in you, He'll give it to you. So far, you hadn't asked Him for a thing where I'm concerned. All you got to do is ask. Then you'll get it and a wagonload of joy.

25-33 "I've used a lot of figures of speech in talking to y'all. In the future, it won't have to be that way. I'll tell you about the Father and I'll use easier words. When that time comes, your communication to the Father will also change. You can ask something in My name and the Father will recognize you without Me having to make requests on your behalf. My

Father loves you, on account of you've proven your love for Me, and because you know that I'm from God. Let Me show you what I mean. See if what I'm saying ain't as clear as the sky: I came from the Father above to this world. Then, I'll leave the world and return to the Father."

"A-ha!" His tag-alongs said. "That time You didn't flower Your words up all fancy—You just spoke real clear! We may not be real smart, but we ain't got a doubt in the world that You know everything, and there ain't no reason to doubt it. This just affirms that You came from God."

"Finally!" Jesus said. "Do you get it now? It's about time! In fact, it's right on time. Y'all are fixing to scatter like a covey of quail. You're gonna high-tail it to your homes and leave Me standing here alone. But I'm never alone, on account of the Father's always by My side. I want you to have a peace about what's fixing to happen, so I'm being real blunt with what I'm telling you. The world's gonna give you 'what-for'—but hang on to your saddles! I've already whooped the world."

CHAPTER SEVENTEEN

I'M PRAYING FOR THEM

1-5 When Jesus finished talking to His tag-alongs, He looked up and started talking to His Father: "Father, it's time. Show them who I am so that I can show them who You are. You placed the hides and hearts of man into My hands so that I can help those You've given Me live forever. They can have this forever life by knowing You, the only real God, and by knowing the One You sent here—Jesus Christ!

"I've honored Your name down here by finishing the job you set out for Me to do. Now, Father, let Me enjoy the honor of Your presence once again—just like the old days, even before this place existed."

6-12 "I've pulled back the curtain and let them tag-alongs You gave Me take a look at who You really are. They belonged to You and You let Me have them. They've done a good job of holding onto Your word. They're firmly convinced that I and everything I've done came from You, because I simply gave them the words You gave Me. They took them and have no doubt they came from You. They believe that You sent Me here.

"I'm praying for them. I'm not praying for the ones in the world that turned their back on You, but for them that You gave Me. They belong to You. What's Mine is Yours, and vice-versa. Others will see Me through them. Folks will no longer be able to see Me down here, but they'll have to see Me through them because I'm coming home to You.

"Perfect Father, keep an eye on them that You gave Me. Put Your name over them like a permanent brand. Hold them together in unity like You and I are held together. Whilst I've been down here, I've enjoyed looking out for them You shared with Me under the protection of Your name. I took watch over them and didn't lose any, except for the one kid that was hell-bent on destruction (which was necessary to fulfill what the Good Book already knew about)."

13-19 "Now, I'm coming home. I could wait and talk to You later, but I want to talk to You from down here because I'm ready for My tag-alongs to have My joy completely installed in their hearts as soon as possible. I've given them Your instructions. I told them how the world's gonna hate them because they're different and the stuff that appeals to the world don't appeal to them—just like it never appealed to Me. I wouldn't want You to snatch them out of the world; I'm just asking You to protect them from the mean one.

This world ain't for them or Me. Make them stand out by Your truth; anything You say is truth. You sent Me here, so I'm sending them the same way. I stood out for them so they could be noticeably changed by the truth."

20-23 "There's others I want to pray for whilst I'm at it. I want to pray for every person that puts their faith in Me on account of the message they heard from My tag-alongs. Draw them all together as one, just like You and Me are together. Draw them all up next to Us, so that the world will realize that You sent Me here. The same honor You gave Me, I gave them. I pray that they'll draw together just like You and I are together. I'm inside them and You're inside Me. You can't get much closer than that! It should be obvious to the world that You sent Me here and that all My tag-alongs and Me are the objects of Your complete love."

24-26 "Father, My desire is to have them with Me, right beside Me. I want them to see what I get to see all the time. I want them to feel what I get to feel—a love that existed before the world was ever made. Perfect Father, the world You made doesn't even know You. But I know You. And now, these that You sent Me know You. I told them all about You and plan on doing it some more before it's all said and done, so that this amazing love You have given Me will dance inside them—and so that I may dance inside them."

CHAPTER EIGHTEEN

JUDAS LED A POSSE

1-10 When Jesus finished praying, He and His tag-alongs crossed over Kidron Creek to a nice garden area. They dismounted and walked up into the garden. The traitor, Judas, was well aware of the place being that Jesus took the tag-alongs there regularly. So, Judas led a posse of Marshall's deputies and others from the uppity religious types and the Legalists, and they came to the garden carrying lanterns, torches, and weapons.

Jesus knew what was fixing to happen, and went out to face them, "Who are you after?"

"Jesus, from Nazareth," they answered.

"That'd be Me," Jesus said. As soon as Jesus said that, the power of His words caused them to jump back a little, and they tripped over themselves, and hit the ground. Judas, the traitor, was smack dab in the middle of them.

Jesus asked them again, "Who are you after?"

"Jesus, from Nazareth," they answered.

"I told you that'd be Me," Jesus answered. "So, if you're just after Me, let these other fellas go." Jesus wanted to make good on what He'd said in His prayer: "I didn't lose any of them."

Rocky pulled a Bowie knife from behind his belt and attacked an errand boy named Malchus who worked for the uppity religious types. That Bowie knife cut Malchus's right ear plum off.

11-13 Jesus hollered at Rocky, "Put that thing away! Don't you think I'm ready and willing to bust this bronc that My Father has set under Me?"

Then the Marshall's officers and local posse took ahold of Jesus and tied Him up. They took Him to Annas, the father-in-law of Caiaphas. Caiaphas was the biggest of the big-wig religious types. He's the same one that said it'd be a good thing for one fella to die for everybody else.

15-18 While this was happening, Rocky and another tag-along were following Jesus's trail. That other tag-along that followed Jesus had connections with the big-wig's family, so he was able to get inside Annas's property and see what was going on. Rocky had to stay out by the gate. So, the other tag-along went down to the gate and got permission from a girl who worked for Annas to let Rocky in.

But the girl asked Rocky, "You ain't one of the tag-alongs that follows Jesus around, are you?"

"Of course not!" he said. Some of the folk who worked for the uppity religious types had built a big fire out in Annas's back yard to knock the chill off. While they were standing there warming themselves, Rocky went over and started warming himself at their fire.

19-24 Annas asked Jesus about His tag-alongs and His beliefs.

"My beliefs are no secret," Jesus answered. "I shared My beliefs openly in the church-houses where all the religious folk gather. Why are you asking Me what I've been teaching? Why not ask them?"

One of the local hombres from the posse went over and smacked Jesus in the jaw and yelled, "Don't talk to any of the big-wig folks like that!"

"Did I say something wrong?" Jesus asked. "If there's something wrong with what I've been teaching, please, I'd like to hear about it. But if what I'm saying is true, why do your thugs beat Me?"

Annas sent Jesus, still tied up, to Caiaphas, the biggest of the big-wig religious types.

25-27 While Rocky was warming himself by the fire, somebody said, "Hey! Are you one of His tag-alongs?" Rocky chuckled nervously and said, "No, of course not!"

But one of Malchus's kinfolk (Malchus was the errand boy that lost his ear to Rocky's Bowie knife) was standing at the fire, and said, "You look like one of the fellas that was with Jesus at the garden when we arrested Him." Rocky denied it again. Somewhere nearby, a rooster crowed.

28-38 When they finished with Jesus at Caiaphas's, they hauled Him over to the Roman governor's mansion. This took place in the wee hours of the morning. They didn't go inside the governor's mansion on account of they had a big religious ceremony coming up and they'd defile themselves if they went into an unreligious type's house. So, the governor came out to them and asked, "What y'all got against this Fella?"

They were a bit testy with the governor and said, "If this Fella wasn't a criminal, do you think we'd be handing Him over to you in the middle of the night?"

"You folks have laws. Punish Him yourselves," replied the governor.

"Well, that's where it gets sort of sticky," they admitted. "It's against our laws to kill anyone, doggonit."

Jesus had been right when He predicted the way He'd die. The governor went back inside his mansion, motioned for Jesus to be brought to him, and said to Jesus, "Are You the King of the religious types?"

Jesus answered, "Are you interested in who I am personally? Or did somebody else tell you this about Me?"

"Do I look like a religious type to You?" the governor replied. "Your own country and the religious types put You into my custody. What'd You do?"

"I'm not really with them. My kingdom is far from here,"

said Jesus. "If this was My kingdom, My followers would put up a fight before letting the religious folks take Me. Truth is: My kingdom exists in a different way and in a different place."

"But You are a king, right?" asked the governor.

"Those are your words," Jesus answered. "The reason for My birth, and the reason for My coming here is to tell the world the truth. Anybody that knows the truth listens to Me."

"Truth," the governor rubbed his chin and sighed, "I don't even know what that is."

The governor went back out to talk to the religious types and told them, "I can't see that this Fella has done a thing wrong. I'm not gonna charge Him with anything. The only thing I can do is release a prisoner when you have your annual holy day, which is almost here. It's one of your traditions that I can allow. So," the governor said with a smirk, "Y'all want me to give you back your king?"

"No!" they shouted, "Not Him! Let Barabbas go!" Barabbas was a scoundrel and a rebel.

CHAPTER NINETEEN

SKULL HILL

1-4 The governor had Jesus tied up to a whipping post and his men laid their whips across Jesus's bare back. The local posse twisted a bunch of thorn branches into the shape of a crown and pushed it down on top of His head. They took an old horse blanket and threw it around His shoulders. They took turns coming up to Him, punching Him in the face, and saying, "Hail, O King of the Religious Types!"

The governor went out to the religious types again and said, "I want you to take another look at this Fella you brought to me. I'm bringing Him out to let you know that I ain't bringing criminal charges against Him."

5-12 Jesus appeared wearing the thorns and blanket. Blood ran down His face. The blanket stuck to His back that had been whipped to shreds. The governor said to the crowd, "Take a look at Him!"

When the big-wig religious types and the Marshall's men saw Jesus, they hollered, *"Crucify Him! Crucify Him!"*

Thunder Johnson sees the furrowed brows on the faces of his campfire guests and explains what it meant to be crucified. "Crucifying was the way they hung their outlaws back then. It was an awful way of dying. A man was laid down on two crossbars. On one of the crossbars the man's arms were stretched out and great big nails were driven through his hands and into the wood. They put his head near the top of the other longer crossbar and nailed his feet into the wood, one foot on top of the other. Then the man and the cross were hoisted up and the long cross beam was dropped into a hole in the ground. Most criminals would prefer a quick rope." Then, Thunder continued . . .

The governor answered, "Do it yourselves! He ain't done anything worth being crucified for."

"But we have a rule," the religious folks said to the governor. "Accordin' to that rule, He has to die, since He's been telling everybody He Himself is the Son of God."

When the governor heard these words, it made him shaky and unsettled. He went back into his mansion and asked Jesus, "Where'd You come from?" Jesus held His tongue. So, the governor said, "You really ought to answer me. I'm the only hope You've got. My hands hold the power to set You free and the power to hang You."

"You have no power over Me," Jesus answered through painful breaths, "except what has been given to you from up there. But don't fret none. You're not nearly as guilty as the one who turned Me in to you."

The governor tried everything he could to let Jesus go. But the religious folks were shoutin' and hollerin' outside his mansion, "If you let this Fella go, you have no loyalty to Caesar. By calling Himself 'king,' He has defied Caesar!"

13-16 The governor heard them and brought Jesus back outside again. The governor went over and sat behind his judging bench. It was about six o'clock in the morning. It was the day that all the religious types were to get ready for the annual holy day. The governor pointed at Jesus and told them, "Here's your king!"

But they shouted with anger in reply, "Get rid of Him! Kill Him! Crucify Him!"

The governor said, "You folks want me to hang your king on a cross?"

"The only king we have is Caesar!" shouted the big-wig religious types.

The governor was fighting a losing battle and he knew it. So, he nodded in consent of Jesus's crucifixion and they took Jesus away.

17-19 With the crossbar strapped to His back, Jesus was led to a place called Skull Hill. He was hung there on a cross between two others, one on each side, and Jesus in the middle. The governor had someone paint a sign and hang it from the top of Jesus's cross. The sign read: JESUS OF NAZARETH: KING OF THE RELIGIOUS FOLK.

20-22 The place where Jesus hung on the cross was not far from Jerusalem. Lots of religious folks read the sign since it was writ in three languages: Hebrew, Latin, and Greek. The big-wigs of the religious folk wanted the governor to take that sign down or change it to, "He said, 'I'm king of the religious folk.'"

The governor said, "What I've written stays."

23-24 While Jesus was hanging on the cross, the local hanging crew who crucified Him took His clothes and divided them into four parts, one for each fella. They also took His hat. They didn't want to divide His hat into four pieces so they said, "Let's draw straws for it." By doing so, they fulfilled the Good Book where it was written: "They took My clothes and divided them amongst themselves, and drew straws for My hat." (Quote from Psalm 22:18)

25-27 Jesus's mom and aunt Mary (married to Clopas), along with Mary Magdalene, stood near the cross. Jesus looked down and saw His mom and the tag-along that had always been closest to Him. *(Thunder Johnson lowered his* *head and paused, as if fighting back some fierce sadness. Then it dawns on you that he was talking about himself! He was the unnamed tag-along).* Jesus said to His mom, "Ma'am, yonder is your son." She followed Jesus's eyes to where the tag-along was standing. Then Jesus said to the tag-along, "Here's your mom." From that point on, he became like a son to her and took her to his own house. *(Thunder Johnson let out a heavy sigh, and continued . . .)*

28-30 Jesus knew He had done all He was supposed to. Even when He said, "I'm thirsty!" He was fulfilling the words of the Good Book. Some spoiled and sour wine sat nearby in a cup; so, they dabbed a sponge down into that wine, tied the sponge to a tree branch, and held it up to His mouth.

When Jesus tasted the sour wine, He cried out, "It's over!" Then He lowered His head and released His Spirit.

31-37 Since it was still the same day of preparing for the annual holy day, the religious folks didn't want the bodies hanging up there on the upcoming holiest day of the year. They asked the governor to have the men's legs broke (in case they weren't dead, they couldn't run away—I reckon), and have the bodies hauled off. So, the hanging crew broke the legs of the men on either side of Jesus. But when they came to Jesus's body, there was no doubt He was dead, so they didn't break His legs. One of them jabbed a spear into Jesus's side, and blood and water came gushing out. This is a true testimony from someone who saw it happen with his own eyes.

That someone is being completely honest because he knows how badly you need to believe in Jesus. All this happened to fulfill the Good Book: "None of His bones were broke." (Quote from Psalm 34:20) In another place, the Good Book says: "They'll look at the Fella they pierced." (Quote from Zechariah 12:10)

38-42 A man named Joe, from Arimathea, asked the governor if he could have Jesus's body. Joe was a tag-along of Jesus, but a secret one. He'd believed in Jesus, but was afraid of the religious folk. The governor granted Joe permission, so he carried Jesus's body toward the tombs. Nick (the fella that came to Jesus late one night) met up with Joe, carrying about seventy-five pounds of burial spices. They wrapped Jesus's body up in sheets, mixing in the spices as they wrapped, which was customary for their folk. There was a garden that had an unused tomb close to where Jesus was crucified. Since they were in a hurry on account of the religious holiday, and since the tomb was right there, that's where they laid Him.

Thunder Johnson lowered his head and wiped his eyes. Without looking at you or the others, he stood, whispered, "Y'all give me a minute," and walked away from the campfire. Within a few minutes, he comes back and finishes the story.

CHAPTER TWENTY

I SAW HIM! HE'S ALIVE!

1-10 Early Sunday morning, while it was still dark, Mary Magdalene went to the tomb where they'd laid Jesus. When she got there, she noticed that the big rock in front of Jesus's tomb had been moved away from the entrance. She high-tailed it out of there and ran to where Rocky and the tag-along that was always close to Jesus was staying. She told them, "Somebody stole the Lord's body out of His grave and we don't know where they took Him!"

Rocky and the other tag-along jumped up and headed out the door for the tomb. They were both running as fast as they could and keeping up with each other, but the other tag-along had a burst of speed, outran Rocky, and got to the tomb first. He stooped down and looked inside. He seen some sheets laying in there, but he froze and didn't go all the way inside the tomb. When Rocky got there, he went right on into the tomb and seen the sheets. The part that had been wrapped around Jesus's head wasn't lying with the rest of the sheets. It was folded up in a separate pile all by itself. The other tag-along, the first one to the tomb, finally went inside. When he seen the way the sheets were laying, he knew what it meant. He believed! At that time, they weren't all that caught up on their Good Book 'ciphering and didn't know that Jesus was gonna get back up from being dead. Those two tag-alongs walked back home together, mulling over the whole list of possibilities.

11-18 Mary stayed there at the tomb, just outside it. She was bawling her eyes out. Though she was still crying, she decided to peek inside the tomb. She couldn't believe her tear-filled eyes: Two of Heaven's messengers in bright 'n shiny clothing were perched inside the tomb! One sat where Jesus's head had been, and the other sat where His feet had been. They spoke to Mary, "Ma'am, why all the tears?"

"Someone took away my Lord's body," she said. "And I want to know where they put Him." As soon as she said that, she felt someone behind her. She turned around, and Jesus was standing there, only she didn't recognize Him.

"Ma'am," Jesus said to her, "Why are you crying? Did you lose someone?"

She figured He worked in the garden, and said, "Mister, if you put Him somewhere else, please tell me, and I'll take Him."

"Mary!" Jesus spoke her name the way only He could.

She tossed her head in His direction with a jolt, and said to Him in Hebrew, *"Rabboni!"*—meaning, "Teacher." She looked like she was about to bear hug Him when Jesus said, "Don't wrinkle Me. I haven't gone back to My Father yet. I need you to go to My tag-alongs and tell them that I'll soon be back with My Father and your Father—Our God."

Mary Magdalene's heart was pounding as she ran back and gave the good news to the tag-alongs, "I saw Him! I saw the Lord! He's alive!" She told them what He said for her to tell them.

19-23 Later that evening, the tag-alongs were all hiding together with the doors locked, figuring the religious folk would be hunting them next. There'd been so much happening and all kinds of talk about whether Jesus's body was stolen or if He was alive. Jesus answered that question when He came outta nowhere and stood right in front of 'em! He smiled and said, "I promised peace, and I'm here to make good on that promise."

They were stunned, just staring at Him. Jesus showed them His scarred-up hands and His side where the spear jabbed Him. It had to be Him. The tag-alongs yelped and hollered and celebrated when they saw that Jesus really was alive!

Jesus said to them, "Peace is My gift to you! The same way My Father sent Me here, it's My turn to send you." After

He said that, He blew His breath on them and said, "Welcome the Holy Spirit inside you. If you forgive folks of their faults, they will be forgiven; if you don't forgive them of their faults, they'll still be at fault."

24-29 One of the tag-alongs was missing from the room, Tommy the Twin. The other tag-alongs kept telling Tommy, "We saw Him—We saw the Lord!"

But Tommy said, "I ain't gonna believe it until I see the actual print marks from the nails in His hands, stick my fingers into His hands, and put my whole fist into His side!"

Eight days later, Tommy got his chance. He was with all the other tag-alongs. The doors were locked again. But it didn't stop Jesus. He came in, stood in the middle of them, and said the same thing, "Peace is My gift to you!"

Jesus walked over to Tommy and said, "Stick your finger here in My hands. Put your fist into My side. I want you believing, Twin, not doubting."

Tommy looked at Jesus in amazement and said, "You are My Lord and My God!"

29 Jesus said, "You had to see Me with your own eyes to believe. Faith-filled and blessed are those who believe without seeing."

30-31 Jesus did a lot more miraculous works in front of His tag-alongs that didn't make their way into this story. But this story has a bigger purpose than just telling miracles. This story was told so that you would believe Jesus truly is the Promised One, the Son of God, and by believing that truth, you will have real life in His name.

CHAPTER TWENTY-ONE

FEED MY CRITTERS

1-6 Later, Jesus showed up by the Lake of Tiberias to surprise His tag-alongs again. It happened like this:

Rocky, Tommy, Nate, Zeb's sons, and a couple of other tag-alongs were together.

"I'm goin' fishin'," Rocky told them.

"Wait for us," they said. They all hopped into the boat and fished all night without a bite. When morning came, and the sun broke the horizon, they saw someone standing on the shore. They had no idea it was Jesus.

"You fellas catch any fish?" Jesus asked.

"Nope."

"Try the other side of the boat," He said. "You'll find a few." No fisherman likes to be told how to fish, but these guys were desperate. They tried the other side of the boat, and caught more fish than they could carry back in.

7-10 The tag-along who was closest to Jesus figured this kind of fish story had the fingerprints of Jesus all over it. He laughed and said to Rocky, "That Fella that told us to fish on this side of the boat is the Lord!"

Rocky pulled his shirt back on and dove into the water. They weren't but a hundred yards from shore, and the other tag-alongs in the boat worked their way toward the shore with a boat full of fish. When they got to shore, they saw a campfire with fish cooking on it, and some hot bread.

"Fetch Me some of the fish y'all caught," Jesus grinned.

11-14 Rocky hopped up and brought the net that held all the fish. They were big fish, and there were plenty of them. You know these fellas were true fishermen on account of they even tallied the fish: 153! It's a wonder they didn't bust the net.

"Let's have breakfast," Jesus said. None of the tag-alongs asked Jesus who He was. They all knew. Jesus shared the bread and the fish with His tag-alongs.

This was the third time Jesus showed up to the tag-alongs since He got up out of the grave.

15-19 When they finished eating, Jesus asked Rocky, "Simon, son of John, how strong is your love for Me?"

"Lord," he answered, "You know I love You."

"Make sure and feed My critters," He told him.

Jesus repeated the question, "Simon, son of John, do you really love Me?"

"Yes, Lord," he said, "Of course, I love You. You know that!"

"Watch out for My critters," Jesus said again.

For the third time, Jesus asked, "Simon, son of John, do you love Me?" Rocky was getting frustrated and hurt that Jesus kept repeating this question of his love.

He answered Jesus the third time, "Lord, there ain't nothin' You don't know! You know that I love You with all my life!"

"Feed My critters," Jesus said. "Let Me tell you something: When you were a young-un, you dressed yourself and walked around on your own wherever you took a notion to walk. But when you get on up in years, all you can do is barely lift your arms for someone else to dress you. And they'll have to help you go places, and even take you places you don't want to go." Jesus said this to give Rocky a clue about how he would die, and through his death, bring honor to God. Jesus told Rocky, "Follow Me!"

20-25 As they were walking, Rocky turned around and saw that the tag-along who was real close to Jesus was following them. He's the same tag-along that whispered to Jesus about the identity of the traitor at the supper.

Thunder Johnson pauses his story and looks down. He starts getting all emotional again.

When Rocky saw that the tag-along who was real close to Jesus was following, he asked Jesus, "What's gonna happen to him?"

"Why should that make any difference to you? If I choose to let him live here until I return, why should it concern you? You just tend to yourself, and follow Me."

Word got back to the rest of them that this tag-along wasn't going to die. But that ain't what Jesus said. Jesus said, "If I choose to let him live here until I return, why should it concern you?"

This particular tag-along that we're talking about is the one who knows this story of Jesus is true, and he wrote it down. He is to be believed.

Jesus did a lot more stuff than this, but the world ain't a big enough bookshelf to hold all the books it would take to write it all down, one by one.

The old cowboy got up from the fire and grabbed a canteen. He took a long drink from the canteen and wiped his mouth with his arm and said, "I am the very same tag-along who both witnessed and wrote this story if you haven't figured that out yet. Every word of it's true. I don't know how I got here or how you got here, but I know it was God who got us here. He must've wanted you to hear this story something fierce. Now that you've heard it, it's up to you to believe it and let what Jesus did for you on that cross change your heart and life forever. He changed mine and He can change yours . . . forever."

The old man poured the rest of his canteen on the fire, and smoke rose up and covered the whole area. When it cleared, he was nowhere in sight. You turned to look at the other three beside you but they were gone, too. You stumbled toward your horse, but she wasn't there. You looked down and your clothes were no longer western clothes from the 1850's. You were back from the past, wearing your own usual clothes.

There, sitting next to you, was a paperback copy of the Gospel of John. On the inside cover, a note was written: "Dear Friend. This is a translation in your language of the story I originally wrote nearly 2,000 years ago. Every word of it's true. Take this story into your heart and let the living Jesus forever transform your life. Your clothing may have changed, but the story never will. I pray that your soul will forever be changed by this true story of Jesus Christ."

It was signed: Thunder Johnson.

THE END

www.ingramcontent.com/pod-product-compliance
Ingram Content Group UK Ltd.
Pitfield, Milton Keynes, MK11 3LW, UK
UKHW022005190726
13853UKWH00004B/1743